To Weston with love...

Getting nostalgic about Weston-Super-Mare

Bev Mattocks

C
CREATIVE
COPY

First published by Creative Copy 2013

www.creativecopy.co.uk

© Bev Mattocks 2013

Bev Mattocks asserts the moral right to be identified as the author of this work

ISBN 978-1493506521

All rights reserved. No part of this publication may be reproduced, stored in a retrieval system, or transmitted, in any form or by any means, electronic, mechanical, photocopying, recording or otherwise, without the prior permission of the author, except where permitted by law.

IMPORTANT NOTE: This book contains a real-life account written from a personal perspective. All the events took place, as described. Everything in this book is the sole expression and opinion of its author and represents her own observations, memories, expression and recollections of events. Other people's opinions, observations, memories, expression and recollections of the same events may differ. To protect the privacy and identity of the individuals concerned, some names, places, circumstances and identifying details have been changed. Any resemblance of these names to those of any individuals living or dead is purely a coincidence.

Dedication

For my Grandparents - for giving me some of the happiest memories of my life. Also for my Dad who sadly passed away in February 2012.

About the author

Bev Mattocks is a freelance copywriter who lives in Yorkshire with her husband, 20-year old son and a cat. Between 2009 and 2010 Bev wrote a blog for the Weston Mercury newspaper's website - a collection of memories of wonderful summer holidays in Weston-Super-Mare, nostalgic observations about Weston and general pondering on everyday life. Today, Bev is the author of a popular blog and a number of books.

Visit **Bev** at www.bevmattocks.co.uk

About this book

Bev Mattocks spent the first 18 years of her life enjoying idyllic summer holidays with her Grandparents in the seaside resort of Weston-Super-Mare. In January 2009, aged 50, Bev began blogging for the Weston Mercury newspaper (under the name of *Bev Osborne*) on a range of topics from local history and genealogy to general observations and fond memories of Weston in the 1960s and 1970s. *To Weston With Love* is the 'best of' Bev's blog - *Weston From Afar* - updated and revised for 2013.

Bev talks about how she learned to swim in the Knightstone Baths and how she went on the paddle boats on the Marine Lake, marvelled at the Model Railway, swam in the Open Air Pool, rode donkeys on the beach, sailed to Barry Island on the paddle steamer and drank hot chocolate in Forte's ice cream parlour. And why she and her Granddad never missed the Weston Cricket Festival in Clarence Park.

On an historical note, Bev finds an intriguing link between her son's school in Bradford and one of Weston's prominent boarding schools. She delves into the history of her Grandparents' house in

Weston. Bev's mum also chips in with her own memories of Weston in the 1930s and explains why she was devastated to find that the new Victoria Methodist Church organ didn't rise out of the floor with flashing lights like the organ in the Odeon cinema - and why the family doctor (who was also the family dentist) prescribed a rather exotic treatment for her mother's pneumonia. Oh, and why customs officers were convinced her mother was trying to smuggle diamonds into South America inside a cushion. And Bev discovers why, if it wasn't for another relative, the iconic Winter Gardens may never have been built.

Bev's Grandfather died unexpectedly in the winter of 1976. Her Grandmother moved to Harrogate to be closer to Bev's family. And the Weston house was sold along with most of its contents. But the memories still remain.

Although it was never her home as such, Bev has always had an enormous fondness for Weston-Super-Mare. The Weston Mercury no longer has a blog and Bev stopped writing for it at the end of 2010 when family pressures took over.

Bev works as a freelance copywriter in Yorkshire. She also writes a popular blog of her own and has published a number of books. And, whenever she can, Bev returns to Weston-Super-Mare for a nostalgic trip down Memory Lane.

You can find out more about Bev Mattocks at www.bevmattocks.co.uk. Or 'like' her Facebook page, where you can also see lots of family photos of Weston: *Love Weston-Super-Mare*.

Wallowing in nostalgia on Weston's hillside...

As a working mum, I don't often get the chance to go away on my own. But last August, while my husband and son were doing the *Coast to Coast Cycle Ride* up north, I took myself off to Weston for a few days.

It was the first time I'd been there on my own since... well, probably since 1976 which was the year my Grandfather died. But unlike the hot, dry summer of 1976, it was freezing cold and wet. However, when the rain stopped, I did what I'd gone there to do - take a trip down Memory Lane.

Actually I was surprised to see how little had changed once I got away from the town and seafront. Suddenly I was 17 again, walking the 'top route' to Eastfield Park (where my Grandparents lived) from Atlantic Road (and Highbury Methodist Guest House where my friends from back home were working over the summer), along South Road and Cecil Road. In 1976, though, I fancied myself as a bit of a hippy and often used to walk bare foot. I think the pavements must have been cleaner in those days.

To Weston with love...

Nowadays - because we live in Yorkshire - I only get to Weston now and again, and then usually only for a few hours *en route* to somewhere else with long-suffering husband and teenage son in tow. But, if time permits, I always take a quick peek at the quiet cul-de-sac, Eastfield Park, walking along to the end to the large Victorian semi where my Grandparents lived for 20 years from 1956.

It never fails to tug at the heart strings. The year-before-last there was a skip in the drive and it looked as if the upstairs flat (where my Grandparents used to live) was being gutted. It was so empty-looking and neglected, I almost wanted to run up and give it a big hug. Cue the tissues as my son put a friendly arm around my shoulders saying, "Aw, Mum's upset!"

Anyway, last year I was hoping that this time the old place would be loved again; that someone would be living happily there and taking care of it. And for the first time since 1976, I decided to take a peek from around the back in Cecil Road.

So there I was, this crazy middle-aged woman, armed with a pack of tissues 'just in case', peering over a wall into a garden ...

It's a good thing I brought the tissues. The back garden, my Grandfather's pride and joy where he lovingly grew vegetables and fruit, had become an overgrown jungle. Like Frances Hodgson Burnett's *The Secret Garden*, you could just about make out the pathways amongst the overgrown bushes, weeds and trees. As for the back of the house, well it looked as if the upstairs flat was still empty. If it looked sad a year ago, it looked even worse now.

Blank, grubby, curtain-less windows... our wonderful flat, home of so many fabulous memories, left empty, neglected and unloved... Yes, the Cecil Road residents must have thought I was completely mad, looking over a wall into a garden and wiping away a tear...

Around the front, in Eastfield Park, the situation was much the same. The downstairs flat looked OK, but the upstairs was soulless. I almost wished for a winning lottery ticket so I could buy the flat from whoever owned it and restore it to its former glory.

But to be honest, I don't think I'd want to cross the threshold. It would feel kind of spooky being so empty. I have strong memories of what it used to look like, much of which has probably been stripped out completely. Without all our furniture, too, it would look strange and upsetting...

So will things have changed this year? We'll be popping into Weston in late spring en route to Devon and I'll take another look. Oh, and if you live in the area and spot a strange middle-aged woman staring up at a house, trying to be inconspicuous, it's not a burglar, an escaped lunatic or a nosy neighbour, it's just me!

The Victoria church organ proves a great disappointment

"Mum, what do you remember about Weston as a girl?" I've managed to corner my spritely 82-year old Mum and get her to talk about the period she lived in Weston between 1932 and 1937.

"Well, seeing as I was only five when we arrived and 10 when we left, my memories are a bit sketchy," she says. "But my parents were always telling stories about Weston, because you know how much they loved the town, so I'll have a go!"

Mum's parents were the Reverend William Hartley Totty and his wife Alice. 'Mr Totty', as he was known, was minister of Church Road Methodist church "although we had quite a bit to do with Victoria church in the town centre which burned down while we were there," she says. "The Victoria minister was leaving and didn't want to get involved with all the rebuilding and refitting so your Grandfather took on the task."

Mum remembers a trip to Boscombe in Bournemouth "where the

architect had built another Methodist church. We went to have a look at it to see if it was the sort of thing we wanted for Victoria, which is why that church and Victoria are very similar.

"Talking about Victoria church, do you remember the Odeon cinema just around the corner? That was built while we were in Weston and it had one of those incredible Compton organs that rise out of the floor, lights a-blazing and all the rest of it. I used to love going to see it as a child," she says.

"Well imagine my excitement on hearing that the new Victoria church was going to have a Compton organ, too. But, boy oh boy, was I disappointed when it didn't rise out of the ground with flashing lights!!

"There was a lovely bit, too, when they were beginning to fit out the interior of Victoria. They put in the pulpit and somebody said, 'That pulpit's too small! Get Mr Totty and see if he can fit into it!' So they got my larger-than-life Dad but he couldn't squeeze in. So they had to scrap it and make another one!"

Just around the corner from the Odeon "on the shopping parade, the curve before you get to the cinema" was the family's dentist, Dr Hewett, "who, curiously enough, was also our doctor. There was an ice cream parlour underneath and my parents used to bribe me with the promise of an ice cream whenever I had to visit the dentist…"

Initially Mum lived at 15 Whitecross Road, but shortly after they moved to Stafford Road "which wasn't half as nice. The local children stole my bicycle!"

It wasn't as convenient for school; Mum went to Rossholme, one of Weston's many private schools. "I started off in the pre-prep at the top end of Ellenborough Park, then a year or so later I moved to their other premises right down by the Beach Road. "It was a big square white house on the corner. In the war it got a direct hit so thank goodness the school had been evacuated to East Brent by then.

"I believe the reason Weston was bombed was because it was where the transatlantic cable came in. In those days if you looked out to sea you could see a post with a circle thing on the top. That was the point where the cable came in. And that was presumably what they were aiming at. Weston had a lot of bombing and Rossholme School was just one of the casualties.

"Talking about East Brent," she continues. "That was one of the chapels my Dad looked after. I remember going out there to a George VI coronation celebration. I joined in with the local children and was most disgruntled when they all received coronation mugs and I didn't!"

While they were in Weston, Mum's mother fell sick with "congested lungs which was probably what we'd call pneumonia," Mum remembers. "The doctor said the only way she would get better would be to get to a warm climate and he suggested they went out to the West Indies.

"However it was the winter of 36/37 and preparations for the coronation were in full swing which meant my parents could have got *out* there okay but would have had problems coming *back* what with everyone sailing over for the big event.

"All they could get was a Royal Mail cruiser, the steamer RMS

Asturias, which went all over the place en route to South America.

"It left from Southampton then went over to Cherbourg. It was scheduled to call into Vigo in Spain but couldn't because of the Spanish Civil War. Instead they went down to Portugal, to Lisbon, then to Madeira, then across to Rio de Janeiro, Montevideo and up the River Plate to Buenos Aires.

"I think the three-week cruise cost £90 in total which in those days was a lot. But it did the trick and Mum got better. There was a bit of a hiccup in Rio or somewhere when customs officers thought she might be smuggling diamonds in a cushion she was carrying ashore to keep herself comfortable.

"Apparently someone had been found smuggling diamonds inside a cushion only a few weeks before and my Dad and the other passengers had a terrible job trying to get the cushion back!

"Mum and Dad also talked about sailing up the River Plate which was covered with fruit, shore to shore. There was a surfeit of fruit, so it had just been thrown into the river and the ship had to plough through it!

"None of this is Weston, of course, but it all happened while we were living there. I stayed at home in Weston in the care of a family friend. I think it was around this time that we started to go to the Knightstone Baths from Rossholme School only I had a bad allergic reaction to the chlorine or whatever it was and never went again. I never did learn to swim."

Finally, I ask her about the Grand Pier. "You know, I wept when I saw the news about the fire!" she says. "I have marvellous memories

To Weston with love...

of going there with my Dad. There was a flea circus which fascinated me! Weston won't be Weston without the Grand Pier..."

So where did the family go next? "Well as a Methodist minister's family, we moved on to the next circuit which was Southport. Then, after that, my parents finally got their trip to the West Indies because Jamaica was our next circuit! Then, of course, Dad retired and he and Mum moved back to Weston for good, which is when he bought number 9 Eastfield Park from Mrs Denning and converted the house into two flats, one for her, now as a tenant, and one for them.

"Do you remember after Mrs Denning died and your Grandfather was clearing out her flat? The bed in the spare room was neatly made up and kept warm with hot water bottles, ready for visitors who never came. A mouse had burrowed into the cosy mattress long ago and made a nest!"

Delving into some house history

In many an idle moment I've imagined what my Grandparents' Victorian villa in Eastfield Park would have looked like, back in the late 19th century. I only ever knew it as two flats. My Grandparents lived in the top flat and an old lady called Mrs Denning rented the downstairs.

Mrs Denning originally owned the whole house and Grandpa bought it from her in 1956. 14 years earlier in 1942 she'd had some architects' drawings made of a planned conversion which never took place, perhaps because of the war.

A couple of years ago I got in touch with the Taunton Archives to see if they had any original house plans. The 1942 plans were all they had. So they posted me a copy.

For years I'd been puzzling about what the house looked like before the conversion: where the staircase went, what the upstairs rooms were used for and so on. Following the staircase removal, the former first-floor landing became a wide hallway with three wide stairs which led down to a slightly lower hall and a bedroom, attic stairs and what we called the 'vestibule' which was our entrance hall with separate WC / cloakroom at the top of the exterior concrete steps. The kitchen, bathroom, living room, two bedrooms and walk-in larder branched off from the roomy upper hallway which was wide enough to be used as a dining room. Light was emitted via a square leaded stained-glass window in the ceiling which led into the roof-space and, presumably, a skylight window.

So trying to picture this space as a landing complete with sweeping staircase always intrigued me and I looked forward to receiving the plans.

OK, they'd been tweaked a little when my Grandfather finally went ahead with the building work in 1956 but they were essentially the same plans he must have used.

So now I could see where the staircase had been and which way round it went. I could see how our 'vestibule' had once been a bathroom with separate WC (still there), and how the stairs to the attic had extended out further before being sliced off in 1956 and boxed in with a door.

I dug out an old photograph of my sister and me with my Grandparents at Christmas, around 1974, in the living room at Eastfield Park. Just peeping out from behind my right arm is the base of a standard lamp, made from the newel post of the original main staircase. A curious relic!

In my imagination, I proceeded to put the house back together again. In went the old staircase; back went an ornate fireplace to replace my Grandparents' ugly 1950s fire surround. I 'knocked through' the arched bookcase between Granny's living room and kitchen to recreate the original archway which would have led into a dressing room which, according to the plans, led through another archway into a bathroom.

Our living room was obviously the original master bedroom, the domain of... who? In a house of this size, was it a huge family with children? What did the head of the family do for a living? Who were the servants who occupied the two attic rooms at the rear of the house? When we were there you could still see the original faded Victorian wallpaper and a rusty old blind that I never liked to pull closed because the room took on a kind of spooky feel when dark. The other attic room had a heavy, oppressive feel about it and I tended to keep out. In my Grandparents' attic I never felt quite alone...

This house wasn't anywhere near as grand as the detached villa featured in Philip Beisly's book *Weston-Super-Mare - Past* with its front and back stairs. For a start, 'our' house was a semi - definitely the 'poor relation' of the detached villa. But it was still massive with a large front and back garden to maintain as well. There must have been quite a few staff to keep it all spic and span.

So the next stage was to find out who lived there and anything else I could discover about the house's history. Not easy considering I live 200 miles away and the house no longer belongs to our family, but at least I could have a go!

More to come!

Living in the Knightstone Baths

I've been watching the regeneration of the Knightstone with some curiosity. Now, like anyone, I know the havoc that the weather can wreak on Weston seafront - and especially the way the 1981 storm transformed the Marine Lake from the delightful art deco bathing area I remember as a child.

So who in their right minds would want to buy an apartment on Knightstone Island? Mind you, I guess if the storms never claimed the old Knightstone Baths and Dr Fox's Bath House, then you're pretty safe. But what a curious place to live… looking out at Weston and all of Weston looking out at you…

And I'm not at all sure about the modern add-on at the back…

But at least everything's still there: the baths and the theatre.

Okay, being Grade II listed helps. I only wish they'd listed some of our older swimming baths here in Leeds. Like the incredible 'oriental and general baths' in Cookridge Street, built by the same architect as Leeds Town Hall.

The trouble with Leeds was that, in the 1960s, everything was so filthy. Thanks to pollution, grime and the way the stone reacts with the air, buildings were black as your hat. Not just a bit black, but jet black.

Compared to this, Weston with its clean, grey limestone was like a breath of fresh air. So were the Knightstone Baths.

Or at least they were in my day. I understand that, before 1925, there wasn't a filtration plant and the sea water only lasted three days before having to be replaced; the pools were then cleaned and refilled overnight.

Mostly, I remember the 'ladies' pool; I rarely ventured into the bigger pool which I didn't like quite as much, finding it a bit spooky, almost as if you didn't expect it to be there because I'd never seen a swimming baths with two separate pools...

Down the corridor to the changing rooms I think there were some individual bathrooms which I found kind of bizarre, even in an era when I knew that some houses still didn't have indoor bathrooms. The idea of people walking down to the Knightstone just to have a bath was a curious thought... At the time I wondered if they were filled with seawater, too, like the swimming pools.

I learned to swim in the Knightstone Baths. My Mum always came with me while Dad took my little sister to the Marine Lake. As I got older, I'd walk from Eastfield Park to the Knightstone on my own, sometimes picking up Granny's friend's granddaughter on the way. I think we went every single morning.

En route to the Baths, we'd pass the long toilet block on the Knightstone with the slogan *Welcome to Weston-Super-Mare* on the roof which my Mum always found highly amusing. I have some curious memories of these toilets being 'manned' by nuns. Surely not!

And of course there were the swing boats and the paddle boats. Plus the theatre and all the other things that made up this corner of the Marine Lake with its art deco colonnades and railings. Not forgetting the Model Railway and the Rozel bandstand at the other end with its concerts, the audience relaxing in deck chairs.

Over the road was Glentworth Hall, which you can still see on our family photos of the time. Not a casualty of the weather, I believe, but because someone decided it was a good idea to pull it down and build a faceless block of flats in its place.

Shame no-one listed Glentworth Hall as well.

In search of Weston hillside's Victorian past

Last summer, in one of my all too rare visits to Weston, I spent a day wandering around the Victorian streets of Weston hillside. If you look past the flat conversions, fire escapes, uPVC windows, dormer windows and porches, you can still get a feel for what it must have looked like when it was built.

I always think Weston is relatively unique. Here they took an entire hillside and, over the course of a couple of decades or so, transformed it into an urban sprawl; albeit a very elegant and genteel Victorian middle-class urban sprawl.

And what I really like about Weston hillside is the way the planners obviously viewed it as a whole. Even though you've got a range of different builders here, the 'powers that be' made sure that everything fitted together pretty seamlessly.

The same building materials are used - local limestone, with softer Bath stone around the doors and windows. But what they've also done, rather than risk an almost military uniformity, is to ensure that virtually every house is slightly different.

To Weston with love...

I love the way it's like a kind of architectural pick'n'mix. You can almost imagine someone sitting down with those huge Victorian architectural catalogues, choosing different window styles, ridge tiles, finials and porches. A bay window here, a fancy gable there... Maybe an ornamental veranda or a sculpted stone panel... The chance to show off wealth and status in the detailing and embellishments... Occupants of detached villas feeling oh-so-much-more-superior than those in the semis....

And imagine the sheer scale of this work, all going on at once. Not just the actual building, but the complementary industries. Metalwork, tiling, carpentry, glazing, pottery... It must have been incredible! Then inside, you've got the staircases, doors, panelling, metalwork, tiles, fireplaces, decoration, servants' areas and sanitary fittings... phew!

Last summer, I picked up a copy of Philip Beisly's book *Weston-Super-Mare - Past*. In it are photos and architects' drawings of some of these wonderful Weston villas. Armed with a photocopy of one of the most impressive, I went in search of it.

I wandered up and down the streets before that *Eureka!* moment in a street near Grove Park. There it was, albeit cunningly disguised by external staircases, additional windows, fire escapes and all manner of later additions. But, yes, underneath all that it was the same house.

I'd have given anything to go inside and compare the architect's original floor plans with today's flat conversions. Here you had umpteen rooms, a cellar, an attic, two toilets, bathroom, library plus two staircases - front and back - not to mention several fireplaces.

In search of Weston hillside's Victorian past

Imagine all those chimneys collectively belching out smoke on cold winter days... And imagine all the servants needed to keep these villas running...

All of which led me back to my Grandparents' old house in Eastfield Park which must have been one of Weston's most desirable addresses in the late 19th century with its handsome villas and elegant private park.

I really regret not having asked my Grandfather, when he was alive, what the house was like before it was converted into flats. But when you're a teenager, you're more interested in other things. My passion for urban architecture came later at university.

I've often mused about things like how the staircase would have worked. I still have a photo of a remnant of that staircase - the newel post which my Grandpa had made into a standard lamp base!

Would there have been back stairs, too? The servants would have lived in the attic, of course. When I was there, the attics hadn't changed at all. They still had the original Victorian wallpaper and blinds and you got a spooky sense of intruding when you were up there alone...

So I decided to do a bit of detective work. To get hold of the original house plans and get a feel for what it must have looked like when it was built. To find out who lived there and for how long. What kind of people lived in Eastfield Park back in the late 19th century? What did they do for a living? Who were the servants?

How did I get on? Watch this space for a future chapter!

Oh, I love (my Granny's) cake!

I've been on a diet since Christmas and was feeling pretty fed up. So today, to cheer me up, my son and I treated ourselves to a huge iced coffee cake and proceeded to eat the lot in one go.

It was OK, but not a patch on the cakes my Granny used to make. She'd spend most of her time in her little kitchen in the Eastfield Park flat, baking cakes, biscuits and pies which she'd store carefully away in the large walk-in larder across the landing.

If I was in Weston, I'd wait until Granny had her afternoon nap and then creep into the larder and go through the various tins like some kind of termite. She never said anything, but she must have noticed herself having to bake more often when I was in the flat!

As a Methodist minister's wife, Granny had spent much of her married life entertaining with coffee mornings and afternoon tea parties.

After my Grandparents retired to Weston, these social events continued. My sister and I were always called in to serve out the sandwiches and cakes while Granny hissed "FHB!" which stood for

"Family Hold Back!" - which meant we ended up with the leftovers if we were lucky!

Granny and Grandpa were regular members of Church Road Methodist Church. They sat on the back pew where there was a built-in hearing aid contraption. Grandpa was quite deaf and unfortunately prone to shouting when he thought he was whispering. I'll never forget the time he bellowed out during prayers: "Good Lord! That woman's hat looks like a tea cosy!"

I remember an occasion at Harvest Festival when my sister and I carried some fabulous baskets up the aisle, lovingly put together by Granny from the fruit and veg in Grandpa's garden. Except Alison tripped and everything went flying. Good thing there were no eggs!

They tell me that the church has been decorated. The beautiful painted Victorian Gothic wall above the altar has been re-plastered and painted over which is a real shame.

I'll always remember Church Road. Not as a very exciting church, but as 'Granny's church', with Granny greeting everyone in the foyer like a Queen Mother figure. I guess she could never quite shake off the minister's wife role!

Granny was born and bred in Bradford, in 1890. She was tiny; under five feet tall. And, like Grandpa, she had a Bradford accent which vanished completely when entertaining, at church or when answering the telephone which she did in an almost regal way.

She loved to shop for clothes, in Walker & Ling and Marks & Spencer in Weston's High Street, always smart and well-dressed, completely protected by a flowery nylon button-up overall when baking her wonderful cakes.

Granny must have been in her element in Grandpa's final posting before they retired back to Weston. Grandpa was Chairman of the Jamaica Methodist District. My sister has a scrap book packed with memorabilia and photographs, even one of Granny having afternoon tea with Churchill.

There were numerous Jamaican mementoes in the Eastfield Park flat. A photo of the last British Governor, Sir Hugh Foot (a friend of the family), various paintings of glorious tropical sunsets, a musical box that played a calypso and a food 'safe' cupboard thing with wire mesh doors to keep the food fresh in the tropical heat and the flies out. Oh, and most of the Chinese Rose Spode tea set Granny used for her entertaining came from a department store in Kingston, Jamaica.

The last time Granny served out tea and cakes in the Eastfield Park flat was in December 1976. It was also the last time I went inside Church Road Methodist Church. It was after Grandpa's funeral and the atmosphere couldn't have been more different from the light-hearted afternoon tea parties I was used to.

At the time, my sister and I were being kept out of the way, lodging at family friend 'Uncle' Joe's farm in Rooksbridge. So that tea 'party' was the also the last time I ever went inside my Grandparents' flat.

When I go back to Weston to have a peek at the old house now and again, I always look up at the kitchen window. Granny always stood there watching out for us when we arrived from Leeds for the summer. I always wish, just for a split second, I could see her smiling out of that window again, tea pot and trolley at the ready…

Postscript

In 2013 I actually made it to Weston three times - and on one particularly scorching hot Sunday morning in July I happened to be walking past Church Road Methodist Church just as the lady who hands out the hymn books arrived.

Seeing me looking up at the church, she invited me inside - the first time I'd been inside that building for almost 40 years…

Yes, the ornate Victorian lettering behind the pulpit had been painted over, which I already knew, but thankfully part of it had been left alone, just as it was.

Apart from that, the church was pretty much the same.

I chatted to the hymn book lady for a while, apologising for not being able to stay for the service; I was meeting a friend in Burnham-on-Sea after lunch and needed to get a move on.

Sadly, the hymn lady had never heard of the Rev and Mrs W Hartley Totty, my Grandparents, who - in their day - were almost part of the stonework.

Sad that…

Delving further into the house history

There I was, assuming that my Grandparents' old house in Eastfield Park had been owned by a large Victorian family: parents in the big master bedroom with its ensuite dressing room and bathroom, and several children in the three remaining bedrooms with servants upstairs in the attic.

Downstairs would have been the large, spacious entrance hall where visitors were received. In the Victorian middle class house this was the place where the family's social position would be gauged. Basically it was a place to show off.

The idea was not only to show that you could afford an imposing entrance hall which was almost a room in itself, but so visitors could 'accidentally' get a glimpse of the even finer rooms beyond.

Here at Eastfield Park you would have been able to see into the house's grandest room, the drawing room, if the door was left slightly ajar. And en route to this room, if you happened to glance to the left, you'd see into the dark panelled dining room. In Victorian times, show was everything.

Delving further into the house history

There was also a third (north-facing) downstairs room which may have been a study or library for the man of the house. From there, a corridor led on to the gloomy and almost subterranean kitchen and larder room plus an outside yard and coal store.

So imagine my surprise when I looked at the newly available 1911 census the other week and discovered that this house wasn't inhabited by a huge family but a 96-year old widow, a Mrs Isabella Hay Murray. Looking after her were a niece from Australia, a lady's companion, a sick nurse, a cook and two housemaids.

It must have been deathly quiet. And I wondered about the lady's companion, 44-year old Miss Charlotte Johnson. What was life like for her? Not the most thrilling of careers for a single woman - left on the shelf, a middle-aged spinster. Was Mrs Murray a delightful little old lady, a pleasure to sit and read to, or a cantankerous old bat?!

Ten years earlier in 1901 Miss Johnson is still there, but there's a different nurse and no niece. Ada March, the cook, and Alice Nigh, the housemaid also feature on both censuses. Go back ten years before that, to 1891, and the household gets smaller. It's just Mrs Murray, Alice Nigh and a cook, Mary Giff. In 1881, again it's just Mrs Murray, this time with a different cook and maid.

As this was almost certainly the first census after the house was built, it figures that Mrs Murray probably lived in it from new. Just her and a couple of servants - how they must have rattled around the place! All those unused bedrooms and Mrs Murray presumably dining alone in that large panelled dining room and receiving visitors in the drawing room.

To Weston with love...

Did the Rev Colin Campbell, the Vicar of Christchurch, Montpelier, (who lived at Highcroft, Eastfield Park, with his wife and six children) pay visits? Judging from the censuses from this end of the street, he's one of the few employed residents. Most are 'living on own means' or retired. All with a bundle of live-in servants, naturally.

Mrs Murray died in 1911 and I've no idea what happened to the house after that. Maybe it passed to her Australian niece or maybe it was sold. This research is for my next visit to Weston.

What I do know is that Mrs Murray was the widow of a Scotsman, a former Captain in the Royal Navy, according to the 1861 census when the couple were living in Wetheral, near Penrith - although by the 1881 census he's down as a Rear Admiral.

When her husband died, Mrs Murray must have moved to Weston and either bought or leased 'our' house. Any more than that, I don't know... yet.

Yes, my curiosity is satisfied. But I must say I'm a little disappointed not to find a huge family living there, possibly with living relatives today.

Other family research has led to amazing discoveries that have taken me, on paper at least, across the UK and the world, finding out about little-known aspects of Victorian history that have been incredibly exciting.

Which brings me around to why, last summer, I was standing outside the recently refurbished Eastern House in Landemann Circus, Weston, just down from Eastfield Park...

But that's another chapter...

The train now arriving at Weston station...

Last summer while on my solo nostalgia 'fest' in Weston, I took another trip down Memory Lane, this time by train.

Between 1958 and 1976, I became very familiar with Weston-Super-Mare General. Before we had a car, we would come down by train, all four of us on the *Devonian* from Leeds which terminated at Paignton, in the days when many express trains still took the 'loop' to Weston. I have very early memories of me at Leeds City Station cowering behind a bench, terrified, waiting for the huge black, dirty, noisy steam engine to arrive from Bradford.

We'd have lunch in the smart dining car with its white table cloths, a three-course meal served by white jacketed waiters. Half-way through the journey the engine would be changed for a Great Western loco and pushed up the famous Lickey Incline, south of Birmingham - a thrilling experience for a small child.

By Bristol, we were getting really excited. Weston was just half an hour away and Grandpa would be waiting with his Morris Oxford car to drive us up the hill to Eastfield Park.

To Weston with love...

By the mid-1960s, we had a car which was much more convenient, but, boy, was it an arduous drive from Yorkshire in the days before the motorways. My sister and I used to get horrendously car-sick...

In the 1970s, you could buy a railway 'runabout ticket' from Weston which permitted you to go anywhere for seven days between Yatton (curiously) and Paignton or Totness plus Minehead (still British Rail in those days), Barnstaple and Exmouth. So every summer we took ourselves off each day. Except Sundays, much to my disappointment! As staunch Methodists, the family felt it wasn't the 'done thing' to go to the beach on a Sunday. So I always felt kind of cheated.

I also felt cheated on 'Minehead Days' when we had to visit Dad's ancient Aunt Eva and sit, catatonically bored, while the grown-ups talked about tedious things. So in a way, we only got five real 'runabout' days out of the seven.

Right up to the last summer in Weston, in the hot summer of 1976 when I was 17, I was still doing 'runabouts'. In 1976 I did the 'runabout ticket' on my own, trying to look cool and student-like and enjoying all the attention from boys!

So I became quite familiar with Weston railway station with its dual row of art deco houses leading neatly to the station entrance. I'd buy comics and books from the platform newsagents and chocolate covered raisins from the vending machines. Curiously, I also seem to remember a dog's grave somewhere with its own little gravestone!

In those days, most of the trains we caught were big diesels with

The train now arriving at Weston station…

proper carriages, not the soulless diesel multiple units you get nowadays at Weston. They had large windows which you could pull open, not the goldfish-bowl double-glazing of today's intercity trains.

I have indelible memories of returning to Weston across the Somerset Levels in the early evenings, lazing back in a compartment, probably with my feet on the seat in front, smoking French cigarettes (shame on me!) and watching the sun low on the horizon across the fields in the west.

Whenever I got back to Weston, Grandpa would be waiting for me in the ticket hall, ready to drive me back up the hill. He was always on time.

So last summer I decided to do it again. To buy a day return ticket to Paignton and stop off at familiar stations on the way back, re-living some of those carefree 'runabout' days.

There's no escaping the fact that Weston station isn't what it used to be. Outside, one of the rows of art deco houses is missing and it's lost all of that neat, genteel approach with an untidy tangle of car parks, roads and new buildings - plus that sweeping road bridge across the railway.

The platform newsagents has gone and the train was a nondescript multiple unit, like a bus on rails, and I had to change at Taunton rather than being able to travel direct.

But despite this, and the terrible weather, I still managed to have a good wallow in nostalgia. But my physical reaction on arriving back in Weston took me by surprise.

I think I'd gone so far down 'Memory Lane' that some

To Weston with love...

subconscious part of me was almost expecting someone to be there to meet me off the train. Because that's how it had always been, every single time I'd arrived at the station in the past.

And, you know, I had a curious feeling of being abandoned.

To passengers arriving at Weston station that Saturday evening I must have looked a bit odd... On the outside, a tearful 49-year old middle-aged woman, and on the inside, a dejected 17-year old girl wanting her Granddad to be there to meet her.

Funny, I didn't expect it to get me like that.

Postscript

In August 2011 my son and I spent a few days in Weston, and one day we bought a day-return to Plymouth. Popping into the station waiting room, I spotted a plaque on the wall - remembering the dog whose grave I mentioned above: *Dandy, the Orphans' Friend, died Jan 16, 1928.*

Standing outside Eastern House, Landemann Circus…

As a dabbler in *Who do you think you are?* type research, I love it when you 'discover' a building where your subject once lived. A building that wouldn't normally attract more than a second glance suddenly becomes intriguing. Call me sad, but I find it really thrilling!

My son's school, Woodhouse Grove in Bradford, is one such place. In fact it was the start of a massive research venture I started five years ago almost by accident when an idle Sunday afternoon led me to some old school histories stashed away in my Dad's house. (What does this have to do with Weston-Super-Mare? I'll come to that soon…)

My Dad attended Woodhouse Grove in the 1930s. But I became enthralled with an earlier period, at the start of the 20th century, and in particular a schoolmaster who died on the premises in 1921.

What started as idle curiosity was to lead to some amazing discoveries which took me, on paper at least, to 19th century France, missionaries in 1860's Africa, the battlefields of the First World War and finally (and here's the Weston link) Landemann Circus in Weston.

So there I was, the other summer, standing outside the huge Eastern House in Landemann Circus comparing it to a photo taken shortly after it was built when the building housed Lewisham School (after it moved from Montpelier and before it moved to its later Bristol Road premises).

It hasn't changed much. The playground at the rear is now a car park. There's also some newer housing on the plot. But you can still pick out everything in the old photo including the house opposite the school which, at the time, was in the process of being built.

It turned out that the schoolmaster I'd originally been researching had an identical twin brother. Both became schoolmasters, one at Woodhouse Grove School and the other at Weston's Lewisham School, apparently as Headmaster (according to the 1910 Kingswood School Register in Bath).

But I was puzzled. Back in 2005 I put a letter on the Weston Mercury website asking for any memories of Lewisham School. A couple of former pupils kindly got in touch, although obviously from a much later era which was interesting but didn't solve my puzzle.

No-one had any recollection of 'my' man, Charles Southerns. He left a position at Kingswood School, Bath, in 1904 and died in 1916 in Leeds, so it figures that he was in Weston sometime between these dates.

Four years ago local Weston historian, Brian Austin, kindly wrote to tell me that, when the school moved to Landemann Circus in 1885, the Headmaster was a Frederick George Comfort BSc. In 1922 he was succeeded by his son, L C Comfort. So where 'my' 'Headmaster', Charles Southerns, fits into the overall scheme of things I've no idea.

Or at least I didn't until five minutes ago when I realised that the 1911 census is now available. Sure enough, there's 'my' man, very much present at Lewisham School, but listed as Deputy Principal with F G Comfort as Principal. So the Kingswood School Register got it slightly wrong. (Incidentally, you can see a portrait of F C Comfort by Arthur Bentley Connor in the Arts section of the BBC website - a pleasant looking, balding gentleman with spectacles and a white beard and moustache.)

What happened to Charles Southerns? Sadly he fell ill and moved to a nursing home in Leeds, presumably to be nearer his brother at Woodhouse Grove School. The building is still there, tucked around the back of Leeds University. He died in 1916 at the relatively young age of 44 from an intestinal condition and was buried in Sheffield (where the family was living at the time).

Discovering his (sadly neglected) grave was another *Eureka!* moment located close to where I lived as a student in Sheffield. He is buried along with his twin brother (who died just five years later in 1921) and his parents.

I don't even know what Charles Southerns looked like. Well I do, in a way, because I have several photographs of his twin brother. As well as being on the school PTA I also run the Old Grovians' website at Woodhouse Grove School and am in the process of uploading a stack of old photographs from the era. Alfred Southerns features on several. I'd love to compare these with photos of Charles.

But the trouble with long-vanished schools is that their records tend to disappear with them. (Apart from my Mum's school archives from Trinity Hall, Southport, which – bizarrely enough are housed at Kingswood School, Bath, as I discovered when I visited Kingswood in the summer of 2013.)

Ah, well, never mind. Maybe in the future something will come to light. Perhaps Kingswood School has something. You never know.

Postscript

In the hot summer of 2013 I took a trip to Kingswood and met up with the lady in charge of the school's archives. Charles Southerns taught at the school before moving to Weston, and he and his twin brother also attended as pupils. At the time the school only accepted the sons of Methodist ministers, and the boys' father, Arthur, (of missionary fame, mentioned in an earlier chapter) was a Wesleyan Methodist minister. We eventually unearthed what was almost certainly a photograph of Alfred Southerns as a boy. On his left was another boy who could be Charles.

Then, one day, I Googled 'Lewisham School, Weston-Super-Mare' which led me to an old postcard of the school for sale on eBay, franked 1909. I bought it and it arrived on my doormat. I turned it over and lo and behold the sender (to someone in Paris) was none other than Charles Southerns himself! Who would have thought it?

Building sandcastles at the Marine Lake

It's funny how many contemporaries I've met who also spent their summer holidays in Weston as children. We probably played on the Marine Lake sands together, or fought over the swing boats or the paddle boats, oblivious to the fact that we'd meet up in later life.

The thing about the Marine Lake is that the tide never goes out so you could paddle to your heart's content all day long. So we tended to go there rather than the main beach, unless we wanted to take a ride on a donkey or in a pony cart.

There was a colonnaded area, under the extended promenade, where you could change or shelter from the rain. I remember it could be accessed via cellar-like steps which descended from the promenade. This of course meant the promenade was much broader than it is now, with red and white criss-cross art deco railings rather than today's limestone wall.

At the back of the prom, near the Rozel bandstand, was the Model Railway with its huge 3D hoarding of an engine emerging from a tunnel. That was still there after the 1981 storms because

To Weston with love…

there's a photo of me standing in front of it circa 1982, so I'm not sure when it finally disappeared.

The closer you got to the Rozel, the better you could hear the music being played on the bandstand, another victim of the 1981 storms. I have memories of a Hammond-style organ playing the Tornados' 1962 hit *Telstar*. I can't hear that tune these days without thinking of the Rozel. Then further around the corner was Anchor Head, still pretty much the same as it is today, with its 'lifeboat lady' raising money for the RNLI.

It was in one of the shelters around there that I remember often seeing the Weston 'bag lady' - an elderly woman who, my Mum used to tell me, had been bombed out in the war and subsequently refused to sleep in a house. She always reminded me of the *Feed the birds* woman in Mary Poppins.

Weston sand was, and is, brilliant for building sandcastles and road systems with bridges and underpasses. It wasn't grainy like the sand at Dawlish or Paignton, or shingle like the Madeira Cove - although judging from Edwardian photographs, when the Marine Lake was still the causeway-less Glentworth Bay, it did have some shingle which makes me wonder whether the Marine Lake is in reality one big man-made sandpit.

In the 1960s you could park easily, right outside the Marine Lake - no double yellow lines! Dad would hire a deck-chair, buy a lurid green lime-flavoured ice cream (always the same one) and sit patiently while we transformed his feet into an amazing sand sculpture. It was the only time Dad would ever wear (bright yellow nylon) shorts and his 48-weeks-a-year-in-the-office legs were as white as snow.

In the early 1960s, we girls wore those ruched waffle nylon bathing costumes while our mums wore swimsuits cut straight across the top of the leg with a kind of 'modesty apron' plus armour-plated built-in bra cups shaped like cones. Bright floral rubber bathing caps were also the rage; the more flowers the better. Amongst all these feminine colours, it's amazing how many men still sat on the beach with plain suit trousers, shirt and tie.

Lunch was always at a café somewhere behind Claremont Crescent where we always had baked beans on toast. In fact we only ever had beans on toast, in every café we ever went to, including day trips to Barry Island on the paddle steamer from Birnbeck Pier.

One year we were thrilled to experience the new luridly bright, opaque sherbet fizzy drink, (*It's frothy, man...*) Cresta, until my little sister drank it so quickly she brought it all back, a bit like the day she swallowed the contents of a whole Barrett's sherbet fountain in one go only to start foaming at the mouth … We were positively zinging with all those e-numbers.

Then there was the even brighter Hubbly Bubbly with bubbles moulded into the glass bottle. And of course everything had crown tops or ring pulls which we'd delight in collecting from the beach and take home with a view to making something. We made some terrible chain belts!

Walking across the causeway between the Madeira Cove and the Knightstone could be precarious. The tarmac was worn away by the sea and was incredibly slippery. That's one thing I'm pleased to see

To Weston with love…

they've replaced recently.

You couldn't miss the toilets - a huge long building on the Knightstone with *Welcome to Weston-Super-Mare* emblazoned across the roof. As I said in another entry, I'm almost certain it was 'manned' by nuns???

When I was in Weston last summer, I spent some time strolling around this area, stopping off for a cappuccino in the café at the Madeira Cove. Along the way, elderly people were resting on benches, just like a previous generation did when I was a child.

Back then, today's elderly folk would have been my parents' age, down on the Marine Lake beach, helping their children to build sandcastles and my Dad's speciality: a fabulous sand speedboat we could sit in.

But then everyone started to go abroad for their holidays. Except us; we always went to Weston. And Weston, like many other British seaside towns, went into decline for a while, not helped by the devastating storms of 1981 which wrecked the Marine Lake as we'd known it.

I look forward to seeing the re-generation, but I'd really rather it was still exactly as it used to be.

Two piers... and then there were none...

You know, I never liked the Grand Pier pavilion, the one that burned down last summer. And, anyway, it wasn't the original pavilion. The original 1904 structure (which housed a 2,000 seat theatre) was also destroyed by fire - in 1930. So every time someone on the 2008 News rambled on about Weston's Edwardian (or even Victorian) pier burning down, I felt like putting them right!

Okay, times had moved on by the time the 'new' pavilion was opened in 1933 and it probably warranted a different use (i.e. amusement arcade rather than theatre) and a more modern design. But I always felt it was 'boxy' and characterless, especially when compared to the buildings on Birnbeck Pier (the 'Old' Pier).

The other summer we walked up to the Grand Pier pavilion and were astonished to find even that wasn't strictly the original 1930's building. The wooden cladding had been replaced with white uPVC. So what you saw from afar was, in effect, a re-build anyway. Or at least a new façade.

For me, the Grand Pier was a noisy, brassy amusement arcade,

To Weston with love...

and definitely not a pleasant tourist attraction (although I did like the Hall of Mirrors and the crazy wonky house). I always much preferred Birnbeck with its quaint clock tower, pavilion café, ice cream kiosk and the steps which zigzagged down to the paddle steamers to take you over to Barry Island for the day.

The trouble was (and is) that Birnbeck Pier is in the wrong place. Not just for attracting tourists, but also because it's massively more exposed to the elements than the more sheltered Grand Pier. And the saddest thing of all is seeing it in its current derelict state. Especially when you remember that in its heyday it housed a funfair and amusements, even a switchback railway plus an additional jetty to the south.

Surfing the Net in an idle moment, I came across a curious website packed with photos of the Old Pier in its current derelict state - very sad and almost sinister, but incredibly atmospheric. Even the original organ is still in situ in the pavilion, complete with wonky keys, as if everyone had suddenly fled at a moment's notice leaving a kind of off-shore ghost town.

So meanwhile Weston used to have two piers and now it has none.

Or at least not until they build Grand Pier Mark III. And from what I've seen of the plans, I'm not impressed. It could be a modern sports centre, shopping mall or office complex anywhere. I think I've seen something very similar on Leeds Ring Road, housing a bank's call centre.

There is nothing that makes it specific to Weston or, just as important, sympathetic to the great tradition of British seaside piers. Not to mention the fact that its position, sticking out into the sea, makes it one of the most prominent landmarks in the Bay. So by its nature, it has to be a splendid, enduring design; Weston's flagship - now and in the future.

Never forget that the 'powers that be' once decided that Weston Technical College would make an aesthetically-pleasing addition to Weston's Victorian seaside skyline...

And no doubt someone will look back on the modern addition to the Knightstone Baths apartments, as it rusts and decays over the decades and people stop wanting to live there, and wonder if the planners were out of their minds.

Now if it was me, I'd design a pier based on the original Edwardian pavilion but with a modern interior, designed to suit modern uses, using modern construction materials.

In a way that would be splendidly more atmospheric than the derelict Birnbeck Pier; seeing Weston's original Grand Pier rising up out of the ashes like some kind of phoenix.

Is it too late to change?

Going to see the lights

Every time I walk past the noisy, characterless bar that used to be the art deco Forte's Ice Cream Parlour opposite the Marine Lake, I remember being taken to see the lights as a child late on warm summer evenings.

That's because we'd always end up in Fortes for a nightcap of cocoa complete with Cadburys chocolate fingers to dunk.

On the wall was a large picture of the devil, either eating, or tempting someone to eat, an enormous Knickerbocker Glory. I also recall lots of shiny chrome and mirrors - retro art deco at its best. Or at least that's how I remember it.

The evening's treat always started with Grandpa driving us along the toll road to Kewstoke for an ice cream (supplemented by Granny's secret stash of icing sugar drenched travel sweets in the glove compartment).

Then we'd return and slowly drive the full length of the promenade to the Sanatorium end, taking in the lights.

Or if it wasn't quite dark enough by then, we'd stop off in the attractive Prince Consort Gardens and sail our little plastic toy boats

Going to see the lights

on the boating lake.

You could see the 'moving' lights along the Grand Pier from our living room window, way up on Weston hill, but seeing them close up was even better. Not to mention the illuminated *Welcome to Weston-Super-Mare* on the roof of the Knightstone Toilets by the swing boats - and the elegant fountain further along on the beach lawns where the lights slowly changed colour making the water turn pink, blue and green.

Was the Model Railway lit up, with its 3D hoarding of an engine coming out of a tunnel? Or the Winter Gardens with its lovely gardens around the back? I don't remember. But I do remember the carefully manicured Floral Clock, near the station, with its huge hands and the illuminated little wooden house where the cuckoo popped out on the hour.

Back on the seafront, the tide was always in, something it never seemed to be during the day. And on windy days, the waves would splash over onto the prom, very gradually wearing away the stones on the top of the promenade walls.

Plus, when the tide was in, the water would flood over the Marine Lake causeway, transforming the daytime mill pond into rough seas. You could look down the steps leading to the colonnaded area underneath the prom and see the sea swishing around, like a flooded cellar.

After our nightcap treat in Fortes we'd drive reluctantly back to Eastfield Park and to bed - and I remember my bed, with its eiderdown, blankets and sheets, being the comfiest bed I've ever had!

The last summer

Most people remember the summer of 1976 because of the heat - the longest-ever recorded dry spell in England and Wales since 1727 (according to the Met Office).

I remember the summer of 1976 because it was my last summer in Weston. Granny was getting frail and Grandpa was uncharacteristically sombre. It was clear that something was wrong.

"I'm frightened because I think my Grandfather is ill," I confided in my teenage diary. "He seems weak - for the first time in my life and he talks like a man on his death bed."

However we still did the usual cricket rounds: the Weston Cricket Festival in August and various home matches at Taunton.

I was in Weston for the whole of the summer; the rest of the family came and went for the usual two weeks' leave my Dad got from the office. So for most of the time I was on my own, free to do pretty much as I pleased without my Mum and Dad breathing down my neck!

Three of my friends from Leeds were working at Highbury Methodist Guest house up on the hill. So on their days off we'd all go to the Open Air Pool, still intact before its disastrous transformation into Tropicana. And I revelled in the attention of boys, some of whom had seen me at the Cricket Festival.

At the other end of the prom, I remember the 'lifeboat lady', as we called her, at the Madeira Cove. The previous year, David, another of my Highbury friends, had bought a thick knitted bobble hat from the stall and had insisted on wearing it, despite the summer heat.

The following week I went on my usual railway 'runabout'. In 1976 I was into pretending I was French. We'd just had a fantastic French exchange trip at school and ever since, my best friend, Caroline and I pretended we were French, feeling arrogantly superior to just about everyone! (Hence the reason I was smoking French cigarettes…)

While I was in Weston we wrote to each other most days, checking up we were still 'being French'. She was actually in France, promising to bring back goodies like French coffee and Gauloise cigarettes, sporting her black leather clogs and lace black acrylic shawl which she insisted were the height of teenage fashion in France.

That summer I walked around Weston barefoot (carrying my wooden Scholl sandals) in my faded Wrangler jeans and tee shirt. I'd been on a strict slimming diet and slimmed right down. I felt fantastic - like the Ugly Duckling transformed into a swan and revelled in the attention I was getting from local boys.

I borrowed an ancient bicycle from Granny's cleaner, Doris, (the kind with a basket on the front) and cycled around Weston and the surrounding countryside. I loved the way everything was so flat compared to the punishing hills of Yorkshire. Except Weston hillside, of course, although I devised an ingenious route back to Eastfield Park, via Worle, which wasn't as taxing as Arundel Road!

I'll never forget Grandpa driving me back from the final cricket match in Taunton. He was uncharacteristically silent. Then he simply said: "This is the last time we will ever do this trip." And I knew by the way he said it that something was seriously wrong.

He'd already been having problems which, that autumn, long after I'd returned to Leeds, were diagnosed as prostate cancer. He was admitted to (the old) Weston hospital for an operation. Mum went down to Weston to be with him. On the 17th November I noted in my diary that Mum had phoned to say Grandpa was "extremely ill and we may have to zoom down there any time". He died the next day.

So the summer of 1976 wasn't strictly my last time in Weston because I returned with my Dad and sister on the 20th December to join Mum and Granny for Grandpa's funeral at Church Road Methodist Church.

But the summer of 1976 was the last time I slept in the Eastfield Park flat. In December we were billeted out with family friends 'Uncle' Joe and 'Auntie' Olive at their old farmhouse in Rooksbridge where we spent the whole of Christmas.

So, with plans already in place for Granny to move back to Yorkshire, I said goodbye to the flat in Eastfield Park where I'd spent every summer of my life.

It's a memory that must have engraved itself indelibly on my subconscious because, in the 32 years since then, I've had recurring dreams which find me back at the flat. I'm always packing my suitcase because it's almost time to leave. And I know I won't be coming back.

Funnily enough, Granny had always been the frailer of the two. Grandpa used to make her rest while he did the laundry, the garden, the driving and the supermarket shopping, taking her breakfast in bed every day and making sure she took her afternoon nap.

None of us expected him to die first. And no-one expected Granny to go on quite as long as she did, all her faculties intact, almost reaching her 100th birthday but not quite.

And, you know, she always bought herself a huge family-sized bar of Cadbury's chocolate on the 22 birthdays she spent as a widow - because 'Daddy' (as she called him) had always bought her a bar for her birthday.

Down on the farm

I see they've put a speed camera right outside my 'Uncle' Joe's former farmhouse at Rooksbridge meaning that if you want to take a photo of the beautiful old building, it's obscured by a great big yellow box.

'Uncle' Joe and 'Auntie' Olive were old friends of the family, probably dating back to my Grandparents' first stint in Weston in the 1930s when, as well as being in charge of Church Road Methodist Church, Grandpa also looked after the little Methodist chapel at East Brent.

No visit to Weston was complete without a visit to their wonderful, ancient farmhouse in Rooksbridge. To us small children, Uncle Joe seemed about 10 feet tall, walking around the old farmhouse with a permanent stoop so he could get through the low doorways and avoid the low beams. He was a fantastic person - warm, friendly and jolly, and always happy to take my sister and me on a tour of the farm to see the animals.

Back at the farmhouse Auntie Olive would put on a smashing spread of home-made everything. Scones, clotted cream, jam… I think she even made her own butter.

Down on the farm

I remember there was a bit of upheaval when the M5 motorway was built - it ploughed right through Uncle Joe's land. With the advent of the motorway everything became slightly noisier than the quiet Sunday afternoons ambling through the fields looking at the lambs and messing around in the hay. And suddenly you had to go over the motorway on foot or road bridges to get to places like nearby Brent Knoll.

My final memory of Uncle Joe's farm at Rooksbridge was the Christmas of 1976 when we went to Weston for my Grandfather's funeral. My sister and I stayed with Uncle Joe and Auntie Olive, out of the way of the grieving older relatives. Despite the sadness of the occasion, I remember that Christmas as one of my best-ever.

The setting couldn't have been more idyllic - like something straight out of *Country Living* magazine's Christmas edition. The inglenook fireplaces with their roaring log fires, the huge Christmas tree and magical, sparkling fairy lights plus, of course, the amazing home-cooked spread on the dining room table for Christmas Lunch.

Uncle Joe was forever proudly pointing out how he'd discovered one inglenook completely hidden behind a later chimney breast and gas fire.

And while he was busy restoring the farmhouse to its original glory, he was also installing all the mod cons - central heating (a luxury we didn't have at home) and a state-of-the-art 1970s bathroom complete with (pink?) coloured suite and a thick shag-pile carpet. Unsurpassed luxury after our freezing cold bathroom at home!

I remember local carol singers doing the rounds on Christmas

To Weston with love...

Eve. Proper carol singers complete with lanterns, singing proper Christmas carols - a million miles away from the neighbourhood kids' garbled *We wish you a Merry Christmas* here in the city.

The carol singers would be invited into the huge cosy kitchen with its traditional farmhouse table and Aga. Everyone would sit around the table feasting on home-made mince pies and other goodies. No booze, though, as this was a teetotal Methodist household.

I think it was on Christmas Eve, after everyone else had gone to bed, that my sister and I stayed up late to watch the TV adaptation of *The Signalman* by Charles Dickens for the first time. Or was it one of the M R James ghost stories? Boy, was it spooky going up to bed afterwards, your mind playing tricks as you made your way in the dark through the ancient, creaky old house.

If my Granny was upset on Christmas Day, her first without her beloved 'Bill', she bravely kept it to herself. My Leeds university student boyfriend phoned to say "Merry Christmas"... the highlight of my day. And Uncle Joe's son gave me a pack of blank 120-minute cassette tapes which thrilled me no end; now I could finally tape all my Led Zepp LPs!

That Christmas was the last time we ever saw Uncle Joe and Auntie Olive. Auntie Olive passed away and Uncle Joe grew old and infirm over the years, moving out of the farmhouse and into a nursing home in Burnham-on-Sea.

But our family always kept in touch. And I'll never forget that wonderful (if a little sad) Christmas of 1976.

A tale of two deputy headmasters...

In an earlier entry I talk about some research that led me to Landemann Circus, Weston, and Eastern House which in the late 19th / early 20th centuries was Lewisham School, a private boarding school for boys.

Like thousands of private schools up and down the country, it eventually closed and - presumably - with it went most if not all of its archives, photographs and other memorabilia, its staff and pupils long forgotten.

This is a tale of two identical twins: Charles and Alfred Southerns. Both were deputy headmasters: one at Lewisham School, Weston, and the other at Woodhouse Grove School, Bradford.

The difference is that where one twin has vanished, the other is remembered. Unlike Lewisham School which closed in the 1950s, Woodhouse Grove is still going strong. My son is a pupil in year 10 and I'm on the PTA.

Before Weston, Charles Southerns taught at Kingswood School, Bath. But you'd scarcely know if it wasn't for a couple of staff lists

To Weston with love...

and an obituary in the 1916 school magazine. There is no record of his arrival or his departure. And, last time I spoke to the school, there was nothing in the school archives.

Likewise, there's no record of him or even the school where he taught on the seafront at Morecambe which was where he was before Kingswood. It's as if he never existed.

Alfred's memory, on the other hand, is very much alive. He is remembered as one of Woodhouse Grove's most influential characters. There is a Southerns Scholarship and a Southerns House. There are also umpteen old photographs of Alfred Southerns and many recollections of him in printed histories of the school.

We know he loved apple pie, was nicknamed 'Sam' and had a print of Barak Obama's favourite painting (*Hope* by G F Watts) above the fireplace in his study. We know he refereed at rugby, played cricket and golf, and brought lessons to life in a way that made them "the most stimulating of all". We also know he was one of the most feared yet respected teachers in the school. If you had any sense, you didn't get on the wrong side of Alfred Southerns!

Was Charles similar? From the obituary in the Kingswood Magazine we know he was remembered as "a teacher of unwearied industry and rare power". But it also says "he will long be remembered by those who came under his influence and felt his charm". If anyone did remember him, then sadly they're long gone.

Charles does actually 'appear' in one of the Woodhouse Grove recollections, visiting his brother. A former pupil recalls how "the likeness between the two was absurd"; so much so that even the

A tale of two deputy headmasters...

school captain got them confused.

He also 'appears' in the archives of the National University of Ireland. In 1900 Charles and Alfred both studied distance-learning degrees awarded by what was then the Royal University of Ireland (a kind of early 20th century version of the Open University), in the same subject. In 1913 they took the same MA, both achieving the same 55% percentage mark.

Standing on Weston station platform last summer, I wondered how many times Charles Southerns had stood there too, en route to the charmingly-named Apperley Bridge railway station, between Leeds and Bradford, to visit his twin. It's also likely that, as a Wesleyan Methodist minister's son, Charles attended my Grandparents' former church in Church Road. Or did he go to Victoria?

Before becoming teachers, the twins worked together in printing, in Wolverhampton. As boys, they both attended Kingswood School and before that appear to have spent some time in France where their Grandfather worked at a woolcombing factory in Reims owned by their maternal relative, Bradford Industrialist Sir Isaac Holden.

But sometime before 1916 Charles Southerns left Weston for good. He fell ill and moved into a nursing home near Leeds University, a tram ride or so away from his brother at Woodhouse Grove and a million miles away from the clean 'healthy' sea air of Weston. He died on 21st June 1916, aged just 44. Alfred was with him.

Alfred must have been distraught. More deaths were to follow.

To Weston with love…

The twins' cousin was killed in action on the Somme. Another cousin was killed in 1918. At the same time, Alfred would have also been receiving news of former pupils that had fallen in action including some of the boys you can see standing alongside him on pre-war team photos.

Then in 1921 it was Alfred's turn. He contracted influenza and six days later on the evening of the 1st March he died at Woodhouse Grove School, aged just 49. Every time I stand in the school chapel I think of the sad memorial service which was held two days later, the coffin "surmounted by cap, gown and hood, and surrounded by flowers" before leaving for Sheffield where he was buried alongside his brother.

So unlike Charles, Alfred Southerns will continue to be remembered even if only as a name on the scholarships boards in the school dining hall or a report on Southerns House thrashing my son's House at squash.

But hopefully Charles Southerns can be remembered here, in this blog, or whenever you happen to find yourself in that curious circular road on Weston's hillside named Landemann Circus.

Venturing further afield

At Burnham-on-Sea there was a merry-go-round on the seafront with buses and cars you could sit in. The man in charge had a water pistol which he used to squirt you with.

But that's all I remember about Burnham-on-Sea. Except the long drive there which took ages considering it was so close to Weston 'as the crow flies'.

Then there was Portishead with its paddle boats on the lake where Dad would take us at least once every summer holiday.

And Barry Island where we'd eat beans on toast (our staple lunch wherever we went!). We'd catch the paddle steamer from the Old Pier and love going down into the bowels of the boat to see the paddles noisily swishing away.

Sand Bay was where my three second-cousins had a caravan. They'd stay there when visiting their Grandparents (my Granny's brother and his wife) who lived in Trewartha Park, just down the hill from Eastfield Park.

Wendy, Kathryn and Anne were incredibly polite and well behaved, unlike boyish me who had a permanent sticking plaster on

To Weston with love…

my knee from getting into some messy scrape or other.

On summer evenings we'd drive out to the *Rock of Ages* in Burrington Combe (and be told the story of the hymn writer, the Reverend Augustus Montague Toplady, who sheltered there from the rain and wrote the famous hymn) and, of course, good old Cheddar Gorge (which, as a small child, I would refer to as *Teddy George*).

I also remember very dull trips to the new (now old) Severn Bridge and to see the SS Great Britain being towed back into Bristol (extremely disappointing as I expected it to have sails, steam, the works - and it was just a rusty old hulk!)

And we always did the torturous drive to Strete to buy our new school shoes from the Clarks factory shop no doubt spending the money we saved on shoes on the petrol to get there - so what was the point?

In the days before our railway 'runabout' ticket, we'd pay our annual visit to Great Aunt Eva who lived in Minehead (another tedious drive). Aunt Eva was my other Granny's cousin and up until recently I'd always assumed she was a spinster. But apparently there was a husband who we never ever saw - except once when my Mum caught a fleeting glance of a man who Aunt Eva indifferently remarked was her husband, without so much as an introduction!!

Aunt Eva was extremely ancient and collected antiques in enormous quantities and then sold them on, presumably for a sizeable profit. As you can imagine, we kids had to sit very, very still for fear of breaking anything valuable in that dark, overcrowded living room!

But Eva never parted with the pianola which used to miraculously play itself, fascinating me. Or the lamp with the revolving device which made one side of the painted shade look as if a house was on fire and the other as if water was cascading down a waterfall.

Apart from that, visits to Aunt Eva were oppressively dull especially when it was sunny outside, sitting like silent statues as the adults discussed boring things, drinking tea out of whatever antique china tea service Eva happened to have in circulation at the time. And the older she got, the more her hands shook as she served it up. (Would this be the year she actually dropped and smashed it?)

As for the mysterious husband... well... I have no memories of him at all!

It took a newly discovered distant relative on Ancestry.co.uk to inform me that Eva was actually married (which spurred my Mum's memory above) - although her married name (Bainbridge) was the same as her maiden name which I never did work out...

Let them eat (a lot of) bread & butter...

The 1911 census is out early, but boy is it expensive to view and download at almost £3.50 a page!

So it's cost me £6.95 for Weston's long-gone Lewisham School (to check out Deputy Principal Charles Southerns plus pupils and staff) and a massive £20.85 for his twin brother's school, Woodhouse Grove in Bradford.

And, annoyingly, with Woodhouse Grove there's a whole page featuring just one person. Hugh Woods of Moseley, Staffordshire, aged 15, you've cost me a fortune by hogging page four to yourself!

But I've forgiven Hugh. Woodhouse Grove's *In Memorium* 1914-18 booklet tells me that "During the British attack on Serre, July 1st 1916, Private Woods was killed by gun fire. His body was found in the third line of enemy trenches..."

Sadly out of the 84 boys on the 1911 Woodhouse Grove census, eight were to die in the war and at least one of the 32 Lewisham boys.

The two 1911 Lewisham census pages are completed and signed by Frederick G Comfort, the Headmaster. However he's got Charles

Let them eat (a lot of) bread & butter...

Southerns' place of birth wrong: Bradford instead of Richmond, North Yorks.

Clicking expensively through the Woodhouse Grove census pages I was chomping at the bit to see who'd completed and signed it. But it doesn't say. I was hoping I'd see Alfred Southerns' signature; he was in charge while the Head was in Canada in 1911.

Anyway, I've done a mini-search on Ancestry.co.uk to find out a bit more about the 1911 Lewisham and Woodhouse Grove boys. As you'd expect, many of the Weston boys come from farming families whereas the Yorkshire boys are from textile or mining backgrounds. Both schools have a smattering of fathers who are shop-keepers, insurance agents and so on.

Ancestry.co.uk tells you if the people you're searching for feature on living people's family trees. And one of the Lewisham boys does - Henry Cotton, born in 1901 into a farming family from West Bradley near Glastonbury.

Henry's son, Allen Cotton, has sent me a copy of a letter sent from the Headmaster in August 1910 enquiring whether Henry will be joining the school as a boarder in the September. He's kindly allowed me to include excerpts from it here.

We see that the fees (including tuition, music, gym, books, stationery, library & sports club) come to £17 3s 10d per term (more expensive than Woodhouse Grove which was charging £12-£15 depending on age).

And that the Head is offering the Cottons a special reduction but on condition that "you will not mention to anyone the arrangement I have here proposed"!

Virtually half the letter is taken up with describing the food. We see that the boys have "porridge with milk and sugar on four mornings a week with tea and bread and butter and jam or golden syrup on the remaining three mornings". They enjoy "ham or bacon or eggs or sausages with bread and butter" and "a piece of bread and butter at 11 o'clock".

Dinner comprises "hot and cold joints", "sometimes soup" for an "additional course", "sometimes fish, almost always two vegetables" and "always pastry or milk puddings". Tea is "bread and butter with jam or golden syrup". Supper is "bread and butter" and "some days cheese". There is an awful lot of bread and butter!

There must be lots of similar memorabilia hidden in homes up and down the country. And in the case of Lewisham School, which closed in the 1950s, snippets like this may be the only things that remain.

There's a website I check out now and again - an antiquarian bookshop specialising in old school magazines. But I have yet to find anything about Lewisham School. There are one or two bits and pieces in Weston Library and on the Weston Mercury website, but nothing about the era I'm interested in, between 1910 and 1916.

Maybe I'll come across someone else whose ancestor was a pupil of Charles Southerns at Lewisham School, Weston. Or maybe someone will read this entry and be able to help. Fingers crossed…

I'm off to Weston on Saturday!

Yes, I'll be descending on Weston en route to a country cottage on Dartmoor. Or if the weather's bad, we'll visit Weston on the way back.

Paul (husband) and Ben (teenage son) have the patience of saints, humouring me as I immerse myself in nostalgia. This time I plan to take a stack of old photos of me when I was a kid in the 1960s and do some 'then' and 'now' photos in the same locations.

And if they'll put up with me, I'll also do my annual pilgrimage to 9a Eastfield Park to take a discreet look at my Grandparents' flat.

I can't visit Weston without going there; it has an almost magnetic pull for me. But I always feel conspicuous hanging around outside like a burglar 'sizing up' a property. With it being at the end of a cul-de-sac it's not exactly somewhere you can claim to be casually walking past...

This year I'll go around the back to Cecil Road again to peer over the wall to see if anything's been done about the jungle-like rear garden.

To Weston with love…

Will the flat still be empty? Last August it looked so neglected I felt like giving the unloved building a great big hug.

And the year before there was a huge skip outside; it looked as if the building was being gutted. I was surprised at how much that upset me.

I really hope all the original fireplaces are still there. And the panelled Victorian doors with their ornate brass handles and fingerplates.

And the parquet floor in the living room. Even the internal wooden window shutters which for some reason used to give me the creeps. (I've never liked shutters!)

But hopefully the flat now has central heating. And the kitchen definitely needed an update. (But I do hope the huge wooden dresser escaped any makeovers…)

I always tell Paul that one day when I'm dead I'll come back and haunt number 9a - and terrify anyone that makes any radical alterations or knocks down walls, and just be a gentle 'presence' to residents that care for the flat as much as we did.

Back on the seafront, I wonder if there will have been any progress on the Grand Pier? Or that dreadful eyesore proposed for the old Tropicana / Pool building? Or the Marine Lake?

And as usual we'll park on the steep Highbury Road near the former Highbury Methodist Guest House on Atlantic Road. Paul will moan about the café on the seafront where he ate the worst fish and chips in his life. And Ben will moan "Have you finished looking round yet? Can we go now?"

I'm off to Weston on Saturday!

Then we will leave because I'll be worried the car will be broken into and all our holiday stuff stolen because Weston doesn't feel as safe as it used to do in the days when Granny wouldn't think twice about leaving the flat door unlocked and wide open.

And it will take ages to get out of the town and back onto the motorway; it seems to get bigger every time we visit.

And I'll leave Weston for another year.

But I'll be back!

It's like having another child!

If you wanted to stop my son from wandering off when he was small you just clipped on his reins and - voila! - he couldn't budge more than a few feet.

Unfortunately you can't do that with a middle-aged man.

My husband Paul is prone to wandering off, happy in his own little world. In fact half the time I don't think he even realises we're not there. And he never wears a watch so he's oblivious of the time. Yes, he has a mobile. But more often than not it's at home or in the car (usually in full view of any passing thief).

He wanders off at the shops, in the supermarket, even at the airport where - the other year - I eventually found him ordering a *pint* at the bar just as our plane was boarding...

I've found myself worriedly scanning raging torrents when he's disappeared on moorland walks - and the sea when the tide's come in, hours after he's wandered off rock pooling...

You only have to turn your back and - pouf! - he's gone. Like Aladdin's lamp in reverse.

It's like having another child!

He did it again on our annual visit to Weston at half-term. He spotted the fish'n'chip shop opposite the Grand Pier, ran over the road to get some and disappeared. And of course his mobile phone was in the car…

Now I thought I knew Weston seafront pretty well. But after pacing up and down umpteen times between the Grand Pier and the Knightstone that afternoon I got to know every inch of it intimately. And the beach, too, as I scanned it for signs of a middle-aged man stuffing his face with fish'n'chips.

15-year old Ben and I worked out a plan where we'd both search in opposite directions. Then one would do the beach while the other did the prom again. Weston seems vast when you're on foot, it's crowded and you've lost somebody.

And I couldn't quite see me going up to the Lost Children's Centre (if it's still there) and reporting a 44-year old lost man…

Of course Ben didn't have his phone with him, either. I was the only one of us with a phone, which was about as useful as a chocolate fireguard when you need to keep in touch.

So we'd pick out prominent landmarks to *rendez-vous* at, like the handy blue painted hotel near the Knightstone under strict instructions to *be there* in ten minutes and *don't move*.

Finally, at least an hour or more later, Paul turned up, strolling nonchalantly along the Knightstone. Of course he blamed us for doing the disappearing act, but Paul being Paul he was pretty chilled and didn't see what all the fuss was about.

"Stay RIGHT THERE and DON'T MOVE AN INCH OR

To Weston with love…

ELSE!!" I commanded as I strode back to the Grand Pier to get Ben… who by that time had disappeared too…

So back I strode to the Knightstone again, stressed out, boiling hot and no doubt a lot fitter than I was earlier in the day. Weston's promenade sure is long!!

And, as if by magic, there was Ben, sitting on the wall next to Paul, both lazily eating ice creams without a care in the world… He'd gone via the beach! Aarrrgh!!

3.30pm saw a still stressed (and by now starving!) me finally getting my lunch - a splendid platter from the Cove Café at the Madeira Cove.

So I didn't really get to do too much in Weston on that visit except get hot, bothered and very cross.

Ah well never mind, I'll come back sometime soon hopefully. And this time I'll make sure Paul's electronically tagged. Failing that I'll dig out Ben's old toddler reins…

I'm just too embarrassing!

15-year old Ben has airbrushed me out of a Facebook photo of him and me on Weston seafront at half-term. Apparently his once-cool mum is now far too old and embarrassing to be seen with.

Last weekend I wasn't even allowed to pick him up from the wild teenage party he went to. I had to text him from the end of the road and then wait until he decided to saunter up at goodness knows what time after 11pm.

It seems that's the way it is these days.

For instance, I do the publicity for the school PTA. I have to carefully pick the times when I put up posters around the school grounds for fear I'll *be seen* by important people like *the girls* in year 10 or the 'popular' crowd.

When we go out as a family, Ben walks several feet in front so any passing girls think he's on his own. Or, even better, assume he must be a student living miles from home.

It's the same when he and I go clothes shopping. It's OK for him

To Weston with love…

to acknowledge me when I've got my credit card out at the till. But other than that, I'm under strict instructions to stay invisible.

"The thing is…" I tell Ben as we walk along Weston beach, "when I was a teenager I used to be drop-dead gorgeous. All the boys fancied me".

I point at the former Open Air Pool / Tropicana. "Boys used to literally queue up to chat me up," I joked, wondering if at 50 I still had what it takes and, having tried on my bikini recently, deciding that I probably didn't...

"Don't point like that," says Ben in disgust. "It makes your bingo wings wobble."

These days it's Ben that's the talent magnet. Apparently he worked his way through no less than three different girls at Saturday night's party.

Meanwhile I'm the one that's so ancient and boring I get airbrushed out of photos.

"Your tummy sticks out in that top," he says looking at me critically.

I say it's the way the top is cut and anyway if my tummy sticks out then it's all thanks to him being such a huge baby 15 years ago. I never did get my washboard stomach back…

"And anyway…" I say, "You don't look too fantastic in the photo either. You look as miserable as sin. Why didn't you choose the one where you were smiling? You know, like you used to do…"

All I get is another look of disgust. What do I know; I'm only an embarrassing middle-aged mum…

I'm just too embarrassing!

But I'll get my own back. I'll put a photo of Ben up on Facebook of him in Weston circa 1995 when Ben was two. The one where he's paddling in the Marine Lake with nothing on but a smile and a sun hat.

Or maybe I won't, because he'll strike me off his list of Friends. I consider it a bit of an honour being allowed to be his 'Friend'. And I like being a 'Friend' because I can keep tabs on what he and his real friends are up to.

As long as I don't comment on anything.

No, that would be just too embarrassing…

I know it's none of my business but...

If you've been reading my blog entries you'll know I visited Weston for a very brief afternoon over the spring bank holiday weekend.

You'll also know that last summer I walked up to Cecil Road to take a look over the wall into my Grandfather's former vegetable garden at the rear of their Eastfield Park flat.

And you'll know that I was saddened at the way it had been left to go wild and how it looked as if the flat was unoccupied and neglected...

I know it's none of my business; we sold the property 32 years ago, but I can't help picturing Grandpa in his shirt sleeves, braces and Panama hat, quietly taking loving care of his garden.

He was a passionate gardener and the sloping terraced garden was his pride and joy with row upon row of plump vegetables plus fruit trees, two potting sheds, water butts and a huge greenhouse against the high retaining wall which backs onto Cecil Road.

He was virtually self-sufficient, growing just about every vegetable

I know it's none of my business but…

imaginable as well as fruits and tomatoes, all of which my Granny lovingly cooked into stews, bakes, pies, soups, jams, cakes and countless Sunday lunches. She made the best roast potatoes in the world - and everything grew in this wonderful garden.

If you walked up the hill and along Cecil Road you could peer over the top of the retaining wall - or through the keyhole of the little high up gate where they used to drop the coal in days gone by.

So I went back up to Cecil Road this spring bank holiday weekend to see if there had been any progress…

It's easy to spot the correct gate because it's rotten, verging on the dangerous considering there's a 10-foot drop into the garden below. As for the garden itself… well, nothing had changed since last year. If anything, things were much worse… and the flat still looked unoccupied…

The large greenhouse is long gone, but the potting sheds which once housed shelf upon shelf of seedlings are still there, now practically derelict.

Where neat rows of potatoes and carrots once grew, and runner beans were elegantly supported by canes, there was a sea of high weeds - a jungle-like wilderness like some inner city wasteland. And the once neat little fruit trees have gone wild, shading what used to be a sunny spot for much of the day despite the garden facing north.

Yes I know it's none of my business. Imagine if a former owner of my house kept coming back, peering over my wall and complaining about the way I choose to do things. The cheek of it!

But the point is… my Grandpa loved that garden and spent

To Weston with love…

virtually every free moment there. He nurtured and tended it, creating something that rivalled anything you will find at a National Trust property or RHS garden.

It needs someone equally as passionate about gardening to carry on his excellent work.

Over the spring bank holiday I fanaticised about winning the lottery or inheriting £half a million or so from a long-forgotten relative and being able to buy back the flat which - miraculously in my daydreams - came up for sale.

Then I'd set my husband to work (also a passionate vegetable gardener) restoring Grandpa's garden to its former glory while I brought the sad neglected flat back to life with the help of an army of tradesmen, interior designers, etc etc etc.

One can only dream…

Heading for Weston - and a fight

"Going on holiday can be stressful for the Over 50s," says the SAGA ad on the radio.

"You're telling me!" I think as I update my checklist of things husband Paul needs to do before we go to France this summer. Car insurance, breakdown cover, warning triangle, GB sticker, driving licence... not to mention all his clothes and shoes, down to his swimming goggles, sunspex and pants.

It was like this when I was 'Over 30' let alone 'Over 50' (which I am, only just!) And it's just as bad when we holiday in England, like at half term when we went to Devon via Weston.

Me, I'm packed and ready to go weeks in advance, the spare bed covered in piles of clothes, toiletries, walking gear and self-catering things.

"*How much* stuff?!!" Paul exclaims in horror.

But I know for a fact he won't pack his things until the morning we go. He won't even have a list, relying on his increasingly scatty middle-aged memory interspersed by "What have you done with my xxxx?" Like he did last time we went to Weston. And we'll end up having a massive row before we even get to the motorway.

"WE NEED TO LEAVE EARLY SO WE CAN GET TO WESTON BY LUNCH," I remember repeating loudly, every day for several days before we went down to Weston, knowing full well that by the time I was up, showered and ready to leave Paul would still be in bed reading his book.

"I don't know what all the rush is," he'd say. "Come back to bed for a cuddle." But I'm too stressed for a cuddle; I'm spoiling for a fight.

"You need to take a serious chill pill," Paul says, "You're just like your Dad". And I suppose I am a bit. Dad packs his bags weeks in advance and it drives my Mum nuts. But even I wouldn't go as far as to pack a bag of different sized sink plugs "just in case". (A throw-back to Dad's days in the Army, I can only assume…)

And, regardless of where he was heading, Mum says that Dad used to pack exactly the same things, religiously following a list his mother put together many years ago when he was still a bachelor. How odd…

Paul says I'm a control freak. However if I left all the holiday organising to him… well… we'd never go anywhere!

But I have a trump card. I know I only have to utter *one word* to get Paul out of bed and busy packing whenever we're en route to Weston.

"*Avonmouth.*"

We've been driving to Weston for years and without exception there has always been a hold-up at Avonmouth, adding at least an hour to our journey. "You think they'd have done something about it by now," Paul says for the 17th year running.

But back in Leeds we're heading for the motorway and a fight. Of course he's forgotten something *really important* so we have to go back and unlock the Fort Knox-like house (four keys and a burglar alarm just to get through the front door let alone into the other rooms). And it's always my fault for "rushing" him.

It all ends in the predictable squabble, fuelled by my regular reminders along the way of the speed limit and the need to leave two chevrons between us and the car in front.

But soon we calm down. There are other things to get mad about. Like the caravanners, the "Middle Lane Owners Club" and the "it could only be a woman" drivers who turn out to be blokes when Paul looks closer. ("Pah!" I hiss.)

And of course Avonmouth when we go to Weston which, in an almost endearing way, will be gridlocked as usual.

But, usually when we're heading to the South West, we make it to Weston by lunchtime. I'll see the familiar hillside peppered with grey stone villas backed by the vast expanse of mud in a seaside town where the (brown) sea only seems to come in at night.

And I'll feel the prick of nostalgic tears as we drive past familiar landmarks like Ashcombe Park, up Manor Road and onto Lower Bristol Road.

We'll park in the usual spot and trot down to the seafront, the warm sun shining and seagulls calling. And 15-year old Ben

To Weston with love…

predictably moaning "Why do we always have to visit Weston?" and jamming his MP3 earplugs in his ears so he can't hear our reply.

Yes the SAGA ad is right; going on holiday is stressful.

But in a poignant kind of way, whenever I visit Weston I feel as if I've come home.

Meltdown at the Marine Lake

In case you missed it, there was a serious emergency going on by the Marine Lake at half-term. 15-year old Ben wasn't just having a Bad Hair Day; he was having a Total Image Meltdown…

So there was no way he was getting out of the car when we arrived in Weston from Leeds.

His hair was all wrong. Just as tragic, he'd left his rock star sunglasses at home. His (positively concave) abs were "fat" and the face wash he'd pinched off me had given him spots.

"You look wonderful," I sighed for the umpteenth time as he carefully positioned each expensive 'putty' covered hair into place.

"I beg to differ," he said in a condescending way, pouting his lips in the car mirror and scrutinising his face from each side.

Honestly, it's worse than having a daughter. He spends more time getting ready in the morning than I ever did. And in my day we didn't have hair straighteners, ionic hairdryers and half the goo, wax, putty, gunk and gel you can get these days.

It was so much easier when Ben was little. Back then he was

content with a quick short back and sides at the barbers. A quick rub with the towel, a free lollipop and he was as happy as Larry. Or if funds were tight, a swift once-over with his Dad's electric clippers.

Now he's taken a liking to the rather pricey hair salon I use. Even the 'graduate stylist' costs a sharp-intake-of-breath-inducing £26... Add on the tub of hair goo and you don't get much change from £35.

The only consolation is that hubby Paul's hair costs absolutely nothing to maintain. He's as bald as a coot.

Anyway walking towards the Marine Lake, Ben was taking a critical sideways glance into every window.

He was pinching bits of "fat" on his stomach and checking if his (skinny) bum looked "too big"... "Do you think I'm good looking?" he asked doubtfully.

"I think you look wonderful!" I replied brightly, worrying he may be bordering on the anorexic. But then remembering how he enthusiastically cleared his plate the evening before and feeling reassured it was "just a phase".

"I'm going to dye my hair black," he said. "Oh, and I'm planning to become a Buddhist."

"You're WHAT?!"

But he wasn't listening; he was busy texting his mates. "They've gone into Leeds shopping," he said, hating being stuck with us in Weston on a Bad Image Day and scowling as Paul takes a photo of him and me on the beach as we walk towards the Pier.

The photo that he later decided looked cool enough to put on

Facebook, despite the Image Crisis. Without me, of course. I was airbrushed out.

What floats my parents' boat...

"Did you see *Coast* on the TV last night?" my Mum asked today. "They showed archive footage of the hovercraft. Remember when we saw it on Weston beach in the 60s?"

Yes, I remember. It was the talk of the dinner table. Maybe it's Dad's civil engineering background, but he and Mum get really excited about this kind of thing.

Mum went on to describe the weekend she treated Dad to a trip from Dover to Boulogne on a hovercraft, then onto Paris by train.

They managed to sneak in a couple of train trips from Paris to various other French cities, typically only staying long enough to spend a penny in the station loo and then hop on the train back. You or I might have gone sightseeing or shopping, but not my Mum and Dad.

But - disaster - the weather turned and the hovercraft return journey was cancelled. The result was a chain of missed connections back to Yorkshire as the state-of-the-art hovercraft was replaced with the old-fashioned-but-dependable ferry.

Worse, Dad would have spent weeks planning these connections with an almost military precision. We used to giggle as he poured over maps punctured with little labelled pins like something from Churchill's War Cabinet.

As a result it only takes a timetable to be a millisecond out of sync and - poof! - Dad's stress levels go stratospheric.

And get this… These days while you or I might work out a route on Google maps and the Net, Dad will still take the train to London to visit a travel company that only has premises in WC1. He'd never phone or use email. No, that would be far too 'modern'.

Yet paradoxically 'modern' is what used to float my parents' boat.

Like the fascination with the hovercraft, my childhood was a string of visits to bizarre attractions. While other families lunched in picturesque country inns, we'd dine in brand new motorway service stations. Not because we were en route to somewhere else but because that's what we'd gone to see.

Likewise we'd go on outings to new bridges. Take the Humber Bridge, for example, or the 'old' Severn Bridge. My parents could scarcely contain their excitement when that was opened in 1966. We were there in a shot!

And on one of the only two occasions we ever went abroad as kids, did we visit the newly popular Costa del Sol? Romantic Paris, perhaps? Or historic Florence?

Did we, heck! We visited Rotterdam, a city virtually flattened in the blitz and replaced with grey concrete skyscrapers of the 1970 Weston Technical College variety.

We spent a week in what, apart from the language, could have been Milton Keynes.

The rotating restaurant at the top of the Thunderbirds-Are-Go style Euromast sent my parents into seventh heaven. It sent my sister and me to sleep.

Meanwhile Mum still gets excited about motorway service stations. Only the other day she noticed a new one had opened on the A1. "So I drove down to take a look," she told me. "But it was the usual Costa Coffee & Wimpey Burgers so I was disappointed."

Why, what did she expect? Raymond Blanc's Manoir relocated at the top of the St Mary Axe (AKA 'Gherkin') perhaps?

Swooning over SCCC at the Weston Cricket Festival

Last summer on my nostalgic trip down Memory Lane, I revisited Clarence Park, the venue of many a blissful week at the Weston Cricket Festival in the 1970s.

How many Somerset and other cricketing 'greats' had I seen striding out from the (now sadly neglected) pavilion, me with my autograph book in hand?

I remember the summer before West Indies superstar Viv Richards officially joined Somerset. He was sitting a few rows in front of us in the Vice Presidents' stand, leaning forwards intently watching every ball of the match.

I also remember a very young Ian Botham joining the team. And how could I forget Peter 'Dasher' Denning with his droopy moustache and (sun-bleached) hair (so sad to hear of his death in 2007) and the tall blond Brian Rose.

"Dasher didn't do much dashing today," I confided to my diary in

To Weston with love…

1973, "It was mainly Brian Rose who did. DD was dead tired, I think. Between every *over* he sort of crouched down on the grass with his head in his hands. Either he was ill, tired, unhappy or praying for a win! If he was doing the latter then his prayers went answered!"

My 'Uncle' Joe's cousin, Bob Clapp, occasionally played for the team (I once went to a Christmas Party at the Clapp's farmhouse, but - alas - no sign of Bob). And last August at a BBQ in Kent I bumped into someone whose business partner is former SCCC player Peter Roebuck.

As well as the SCCC players, there were visiting 'greats' like Clive Lloyd, Denis Lillee (although I think that was at Taunton) and others. Someone (I think it may have been Clive Lloyd) knocked a ball for six right over the road and into the adjoining park taking the elderly bowls players by surprise.

A committed cricket fanatic, my Grandpa watched Somerset all summer long, every summer - at Taunton, Glastonbury, Bath, Yeovil and of course Weston, sporting his Panama hat and armed with his packed lunch in a rectangular cream tin box and his Thermos flask… or, more often than not, a large mackintosh. Plus a radio and an earplug so he could listen to the Test Match at the same time which must have been confusing!

Somerset was the only (?) county cricket team where you could pay extra to be a Vice President so we always sat in the VPs' stand, often alongside players' wives like Mrs Denning.

"My Grandfather is a Vice President of Somerset County Cricket Club" never failed to impress Yorkshire cricket lovers unaware that anyone could become a Somerset VP if they coughed up the cash!

So there I was, between the years of 1973 (aged 14) and 1976, carrying my sandwiches and flask accompanied by Grandpa and his elderly friends, Mrs Taylor and Mr & Mrs Readman. Granny came along when she felt up to it; she was an avid cricket fan, too. So was my Mum. My Dad, however, had no interest in the game whatsoever.

The long, hot summer of 1976 was my last Weston Cricket Festival. As usual, I wrote about it in my teenage diary. "I cannot help but like Ian B. He is SO good looking. Yesterday he was wearing a base-ball shirt and blue football shorts… and was sitting with Brian Rose on the back row of the Vice Presidents' stand with his bare legs slung over the seat in front… I have not yet seen the lucky Mrs Botham."

In fact my teenage diary is packed with descriptions of Weston cricket plus various paraphernalia like my 1973 junior membership card (which cost the princely sum of £1.50 for the entire season; these days Under 16's pay a fiver just for one game).

While other teenagers worshipped pop idols like David Cassidy and Donny Osmond, I swooned over the likes of Denning and Rose (even wrote silly poems about them in my diary which I'm too embarrassed to transcribe here..!) plus any opposition team members under the age of 25.

One player that deserved special mention in my 1973 diary was Sussex player Geoff Greenidge with his pop star good looks. "Oh oh oh! Apollo (what I call G Greenidge) is fantastic," I ranted. "I had eyes for no-one else! Faint! Oh! Sigh! He's tall, slim with suntanned skin, brown eyes, fairly long dark brown hair with a fringe, a lovely smile which he uses a lot, whiter-than-white teeth, thin arms, long fingers, etc etc. He's a fantastic cricketer too! Oh! Sigh! I call him Apollo because of his face and his Greek profile (i.e. a straight, beautifully set, accurately set nose). It's a sort of Donny Osmond smile that he has."

Talking about the opposition... Grandpa always had a bit of a dilemma. As a dyed-in-the-wool Yorkshireman where did his allegiances lie when Somerset played Yorkshire? Yorkshire, I feel certain, but he really was rather passionate about Somerset. And definitely for more solid and worthy reasons than the teenage me with my dishy cricket idols!

Clarence Park was an incredibly 'cosy' friendly cricket ground with an almost village-green-like atmosphere. You could get really close to the players and see the action without feeling you were miles away. And, boy, did I tremble with nerves (or was it adoration?) when I badgered players for their autographs outside the pavilion! ("DD has actually *held* the pen I'm writing my diary with now," I rambled on in my 1970s teenage diary.)

Back in Yorkshire, I'd always go and see Somerset when they were playing Yorkshire. But huge cricket grounds like Headingley were so impersonal - although I do have a fantastic photo of a youthful Ian Botham playing for Somerset against Yorkshire at the more Weston-like Harrogate ground in 1977.

As for whether or not my cricket passion continued after this period? Unfortunately, no. These days it bores me rigid.

My husband has no sense of time

"Watches!" Paul exclaims, rubbing his hands with glee in Weston's High Street.

According to Yell.com there are 19 jewellery shops in Weston and that doesn't include Argos, etc. So walking through Weston last summer, my husband was in seventh heaven.

He has watches that double up as stop watches and alarm clocks and pointlessly tell you the time on the other side of the world.

He has watches that calculate calories, offer waterproofing to a ridiculous depth and monitor your heart rate plus useless twiddly bits that do goodness knows what.

He has drawers full of the darn things, all with their batteries running down together.

As a result he is drawn towards jewellery shops like a magnet. And of course duty free shops are a nightmare with their glittering array of time-pieces tempting him to part with his Euros before he's even left the UK.

Paul is like a magpie. All that glitters (and ticks) has to be bought *now!* I have to physically steer him away. "You don't need any more watches!"

But the curious thing is, Paul rarely wears any of his watches. Or if he does, it's just the same old watch he's been wearing for years.

You see, my husband feels he doesn't need a watch. He has no sense of time.

Now, my family are avid time-keepers. We're never, ever late. In fact most of the time we're too early. My parents have been known to arrive at the airport at 7am when the checkout desk doesn't open till late afternoon.

The Osbornes, on the other hand, live dangerously. Missing holiday flights is second nature. They have zero sense of time and even less sense of urgency.

When we pay them a visit, getting out of the house to go anywhere is a nightmare. Normally we make it by late afternoon, if we're lucky.

Mealtimes are haphazard, taking place whenever anyone gets around to it with breakfast, lunch and tea sometimes merging into one. And they rarely get to bed before 1 or 2am, whereas I'm ready for the Land of Nod by News at Ten.

The trouble is, Paul takes after his parents and I take after mine. Add the two together and you have an explosive combination. I don't swig 'rescue remedy' before we go on holiday because I'm nervous of flying; I take it because I'm nervous we won't even make it onto the plane.

But, as I've said already, Paul rarely wears a watch. And he never,

ever wears one on holiday. So the other year I devised a cunning and very successful plan.

Fed up to the back teeth with the stress and shouting involved in getting to the ferry / airport / train, I put my watch forward an hour. So now we always get to places in excellent time.

And, because Paul never takes note of the time on public clocks, even when admiring watches in duty free shops or on Weston High Street, he has no idea to this day that I do it!

Oh, and what does Paul want for Christmas?

You've guessed it…

I wanted to work at Highbury Methodist Guest House!

My friend's dad was responsible for the bundle of Methodist Guest Houses up and down the British coastline. There were Methodist Guild Holiday Homes, too, but generally these weren't felt to be as 'up market' as the Methodist Guest Houses, and anyway, they weren't anything to do with my friend's dad.

All the teenagers at our church, including me, wanted to work at a Methodist Guest House for the school summer holidays. But I was never offered the chance, maybe because I was lucky enough to have grandparents at the seaside whereas the others didn't.

The first thing I'd do on arriving in Weston in my mid-teens would be to get in touch with whichever of my friends were working at Highbury, Weston's Methodist Guest House on Atlantic Road.

In 1975 it was Wendy and her brother David. In summer 1976 it was my friends Jean and Helen. Others, like Jean's sister Margaret, could be working at the Park Hotel in Paignton, so I'd pop in and see

I wanted to work at Highbury Methodist Guest House!

them, too, on my railway 'runabout' trips.

I'd go around Weston with the Highbury crowd on their afternoons off and visit them in the evenings, always feeling a little on the fringe of things and a bit left out. Working at Highbury seemed such an exciting way to spend the summer - and you got paid for it. Pence, really, but it was better than nothing. How I wished I could work there too!

Of course there were other teenagers from other Methodist churches, made all the more interesting when those teenagers were good-looking boys. Although by the time I turned up, everyone had usually paired off - so once again, I missed out!

On summer afternoons you'd often see a boisterous group of teenagers heading down Highbury Road to the beach, visiting the 'lifeboat lady' at Anchor Head (oops I said 'Madeira Cove' in other entries). *(Question: When does it stop being the Madeira Cove and become Anchor Head - and vice versa?)*

There's a photo of us all in 1975 sitting at Anchor Head with guitars, a long-haired 'hippy' David in his knitted woolly hat, care of the lifeboat lady's stall. I'm as brown as a berry, having just returned from three weeks in Provence, and wearing some very wide brush denim Brutus jeans, impossibly high platform shoes (a nightmare when negotiating the Anchor Head shingle!) and a striped cheesecloth blouse.

Normally the Highbury residents would walk down to Church Road Methodist Church *en masse* on Sunday mornings. Our Leeds crowd didn't, though, preferring Milton Baptist Church because it

To Weston with love...

was more 'evangelical'. I walked with them all the way to Milton each Sunday evening, much to my Grandparents' disappointment, although the older I got the more I questioned religion. In fact by 1976 I'd really given it all up.

Already in 1975 I was feeling embarrassed when the Highbury crowd sang boisterous evangelical songs on the beach at Anchor Head, accompanied by guitars, hoping I wouldn't be seem by any of the boys I fancied from the Weston Cricket Festival. But I put up with it, mainly because I fancied one of the Highbury boys even more!

Methodist Guest Houses always had a 'Host' - a Methodist minister whose job it was to look after everyone for a couple of weeks before another took over. Off-peak, my Grandfather often stood in as Host at Highbury.

There was also a younger 'Social Secretary', usually a student, who organised events like day trips, concerts and sing-alongs - like a kind of holiday rep. Highbury had its own single-storey concert room which you can still on the corner of Atlantic Road and Highbury Road, now converted into apartments.

Each MGH also had its own permanent staff: a Manageress and Deputy plus some full-time kitchen staff. I remember all this from the holidays we spent at the Park Hotel in Paignton where the Manageress was an incredibly beautiful woman who looked just like Nicola Pagett in *Upstairs Downstairs*.

MGH's were old-fashioned full-board hotels, serving traditional fare (announced by a large gong in the hall), even afternoon tea with cakes. There were no *ensuites* of course; just very basic shared bathrooms. And if the guests' bedroom décor was sparse, the teenage workers' bedrooms were even worse with several beds crammed into dormitory-style rooms At Highbury they were at the back which was north-facing and very gloomy, verging on the depressing. But that never seemed to bother any of the Leeds crowd.

I don't know when Highbury finally closed its doors (it's now private apartments) but I expect it became a victim of foreign package holidays plus dwindling church numbers. And I can't find anything on the internet about Methodist Guest Houses which is a shame.

The Methodist Church was always a very sociable institution. You worshipped together, you socialised together and you holidayed together - a concept that seems alien in today's independent and increasingly secular world.

Yet it's a concept that's also quite comforting in a way. You could go on holiday, or work, in a Methodist Guest House anywhere and you instantly felt amongst friends. There was always someone who knew someone you knew.

Put simply, everyone was friendly, sociable and had a jolly good old-fashioned time. The Butlins of middle-class Methodism, if you like…

Free parking at the seaside?

Dipping into the midweek edition of the Weston Mercury I notice that some people are petitioning the Government to drop VAT to 5% on tourist-related activities.

They reckon it's cheaper to holiday abroad than it is to take summer holidays in the UK.

But it's true. Visiting a Eurozone seaside resort can be cheaper.

Take, for example, car parking.

One thing I always notice about France is that, virtually everywhere you go, it's pretty easy to park your car.

It's also almost always free. Although there's the odd pay-and-display, it's often easy to get a free parking space, sometimes directly on the beach.

In fact the furthest we've ever had to walk from a free car park to the beach is across the road. And that was on a fantastic beach near St Tropez! Plus, these car parks have been of first-rate quality which is more than can be said for some of those in the UK.

In France you won't find miles of double yellow lines, either. You can park in places that would have British town councils slapping on a parking ticket before you could say *wheel clamp*.

And in large tourist towns where you do have to pay to park I've even seen 'parking amnesties' where the generous town council waivers parking charges during the peak summer months.

Imagine that happening here. Our councils see the summer as an opportunity to charge more, not less!

At the time of writing it costs £6 to park all day on Weston seafront in the summer, but only £3 in winter. So if you park every day for your fortnight's summer holiday you'd be £84 out of pocket.

Park in the equivalent resort in France and you'd have £84 to spend on other things.

So why, in our experience, is parking at the seaside generally free in France?

Well my (totally unscientific) theory is that it's because the French always break for lunch. Unlike us Brits, they don't spend the whole day on the beach hanging onto their little square yard of windshield staked-out territory for dear life.

Instead they'll disappear at lunchtime and return home or drive to a restaurant. So if they had to pay for parking in the morning and then again in the afternoon, there'd be a riot. They'd be blockading the Channel Ports in no time!

Of course there's the argument that pay-and-displays discourage misuse of parking spaces. And the other that someone somewhere has to pay for the beach front car parks and why should it be the locals who may not use them?

To Weston with love...

But the counter argument is that it drives people to park for free in residential streets to the irritation of the locals.

And don't you think the sea of P&D car parks might be part of the reason why people stay away?

Dropping VAT to 5% might make the seaside more attractive in Britain. Oh, and five months of unbroken warm sunshine. (Plus, in Weston's case, doing a King Canute-in-Reverse and getting the tide to come in more during the daytime.) (And turn crystal clear and blue.)

But in my opinion convenient free parking on the seafront would help.

Here's to the Great British Public Loo!

If the French do free seaside parking well then British resorts must be the kings of the public convenience. Especially Weston which I notice won not one but two Loo of the Year Awards in 2008. (OK, yes I accept that pay-and-display parking might be paying for these wonderful public conveniences.)

I was pondering this on the beach in France the other week. There I was surrounded by mile after mile of top-quality Weston-style sand with a roaring Atlantic ocean beckoning the bathers in.

The only problem was that a good proportion of them weren't going in for a swim; they were going in for a wee.

And those that boycotted the ocean were obviously heading for the pine woods behind the beach, a minefield of tissue and even more disgusting deposits...

But what choice do you have when there are miles of beaches with zero facilities? The point is... when you have to go you have to go. But providing good or indeed any seaside toilets isn't something the French seem to do very well.

Or when they do, they're so dreadful that nipping behind a tree can seem like the more attractive option.

In France I dehydrate. Not because of the heat but because I daren't drink any liquids before I head for the beach - in a bid to last out until we can find a half-decent loo in a supermarket or bar.

And even they can be pretty abysmal and invariably unisex. (French supermarkets should take a tip from Overall 2008 UK Loo of the Year Award Winner ASDA!)

Top attractions, too, can be let down by their loos. The 'Ladies' at one of France's biggest chateaux was a disgrace compared to the kind of loos you'd find at, say, a British National Trust property.

But surely anything is better than the positively medieval 'squat toilet' - little more than a hole in the ground with a couple of 'footprints' for your feet.

I was astonished to find that in the 21st century the French still build this kind of toilet. They're on the motorways, they're on the beaches (those with toilets), they're everywhere - brand spanking new and just waiting for us Brits to aim wrong and wish we'd crossed our legs and waited.

Of course one could argue that different cultures do things differently. And the hole-and-footprints combo might suit French ladies and gents very nicely - so who are we to criticise?

But surely the other culture of merrily relieving yourself wherever you happen to be… beach… wood… roadside… car park isn't just unpleasant and disgusting; it's unhygienic. Especially down south where it can go for months without rain.

I remember my French pen-friend's dad in the 1970s wildly waving his arms around and joyfully exclaiming "Dans la nature! Dans la nature!" whenever I said I needed to 'go'.

30 years on, things don't seem to have changed.

Last summer for example we were loading shopping into the car at a French supermarket when the bloke next to us got out of his car, faced the hedge and had a wee in full view of everyone.

At a stunning beauty spot in Brittany, the French, Dutch and Belgians were all at it, despite the fact there was a public WC in the car park.

Worse, this year we stopped off at a seaside town near Calais where, at the side of the beach, we saw a man crouched in the bushes very publicly having more than just a wee…

So well done British resorts like Weston for their award-winning public conveniences. It's one thing we Brits do really, really well.

And you don't appreciate just how well until you're faced with one of those holes in the ground… if you're 'lucky enough' to find any public facilities at all…

So, OK, if pay-and-display parking is helping to pay for our council-run British public toilets, then I accept that it's a price worth paying!

B&Bs don't get more depressing than this...

I'm glad to see *The Hotel Inspector* is back on Channel 5. I remember when she visited an ailing guest house in Weston a few years back.

Judging from my experience of trying to find a decent B&B in Weston last summer that was just the tip of the iceberg…

Last August I visited Weston for a solo trip down Memory Lane without the hassle of husband and teenage son in tow.

I wanted a B&B within handy walking distance of the seafront. But, boy, was it difficult to find anything that wasn't stuck in a 1970s or 80s time warp.

Or with an interior that looked as if every souvenir from every holiday in Benidorm since 1970 was on display.

Eventually I found something near Ellenborough Park which, from the website pics and description, didn't look too bad.

Yes, the owner was very welcoming and the breakfast was OK. But the room itself was monumentally depressing, made doubly worse when you're on your own.

It was dated, tired and shabby with woodchip wallpaper, a

violently patterned threadbare carpet, rickety furniture, gloomy cobwebbed ceiling pendant, lack-lustre tea & coffee tray and an old portable telly.

The equally ancient divan bed felt damp and there were woodlice nestling in the well-worn sheets. Everything about it shouted *cheap*. The only thing that wasn't was the price I was paying per night.

So there I sat each evening in this depressing little room which, worryingly, was the best of the bunch when searching for B&Bs in Weston on the Net.

The other summer we stayed in a B&B in the New Forest. The room was comfortable, cosy and cheerful, imaginatively furnished with a flat-screen TV, the thoughtful addition of a well-stocked bookshelf, and a huge tea and coffee tray laden with hand-baked biscuits, fresh fruit and mineral water.

The mattresses were top-notch memory foam (sublimely comfortable) and the ensuite was stocked with high quality toiletries. Plus, the three windows overlooked a picturesque village green.

At breakfast everything, right down to the croissants and bread, was home-made or locally produced. Course after mouth-watering course kept appearing in front of our eyes. It was a gourmet's paradise.

And, you know, it only cost us a couple of pounds more per night than the Weston B&B…

Get my point?

Suddenly the Winter Gardens look different...

All those years holidaying in Weston, admiring the elegant Winter Gardens, and I never, ever knew that my Great Uncle (on my Dad's side) was responsible for much of it. Wow!

I mean, he wasn't even a local man (he was Lancashire born and bred). Nor did he have any particular connection with Weston, unlike my Mum's side of the family. So I was doubly surprised!

Great Uncle Thomas H Mawson (1881-1933) was one of the leading landscape architects of his day, in demand by the crowned heads of Europe, city corporations worldwide and leading industrialists - people like Lord Leverhulme and Andrew Carnegie.

Plus, it appears, Weston Urban District Council.

Basically, if you wanted a stupendous state-of-the-art garden, you called in Great Uncle Mawson. He was the Capability Brown of his day.

Doing a search on Thomas Mawson, Google throws up: "Layout

of Rogersfield [Marine Garden etc.] at Weston-Super-Mare, Somerset and alterations to pavilion at Weston-Super-Mare." But that's all.

So the other week I emailed Weston Library's Nicki Bobbette who's been absolutely brilliant, sending me stacks of photocopies of documents and local newspaper reports from the 1920s when the Winter Gardens were built.

Looking at the press reports, I had to giggle because there was obviously a bit of rivalry going on between the Weston-Super-Mare Gazette and the Weston Mercury - the former eager to point out that its 22-page souvenir issue commemorating the opening of the Winter Gardens was "the biggest and best newspaper ever published in the town... a notable achievement in local journalism... much more complete than any other newspaper can attempt to produce".

Of course the Mercury produced its own souvenir supplement on the same day. At the foot of the front page it claims to be "one of the finest Advertising Mediums in the County of Somerset, having a Weekly Circulation More Than Double [underlined!] that of any other Newspaper published in the Weston-Super-Mare Division".

"Put that in your pipe and smoke it!" I imagine the Mercury shouting at the Gazette across the newsstands.

"Pah! Our supplement's a zillion times bigger and better than yours!" I imagine the sneering reply.

Meanwhile it seems that anyone who was anyone was at the grand opening on Thursday 14th July 1925 - all the *big cheeses* from the area with a procession of Lord Mayors, Mayors and Chairmen of Councils all wearing their posh regalia and chains of office.

To Weston with love...

Great Uncle's eldest son, Edward P Mawson, is pictured presenting a golden key to Sir Ernest Palmer, the Deputy Chairman of the Great Western Railway Co, with which to open the new pavilion.

The actual gardens (including colonnades, lily pond, tennis courts, putting green, etc) were the work of the Mawson firm (subject to the usual client tweaks you get with any project).

But how much involvement they had in the design and build of the pavilion itself is difficult to tell. From the info it looks as if it was a joint effort between the Mawsons and various enthusiastic members of the Council. But I might be wrong.

Curiously the actual design (minus the dome) was said to have been inspired by the Council Chairman noticing an illustration of the Bank of England on a pound note, although personally I can't see the likeness.

And the low profiled dome we all know so well has a low profile purely and simply because the Royal Hotel didn't want it to spoil their guests' views!

More on the Winter Gardens later...

What if Weston STILL had the second busiest airport in the country?

In the mid-1920s, the must-have accessory for any modern seaside resort was an aerodrome. Resorts like Blackpool and Skegness had leapt onto the bandwagon. And by 1928 Weston Council was toying with the idea, too.

So they called in the consultants who, by pure coincidence, happened to be my Great Uncle Thomas Mawson's firm - the people that designed and built much of Weston's Winter Gardens.

Okay so gardens aren't exactly the same as airports, but it seems the Mawsons knew a thing or two about the new-fangled craze of flying. And if you think about it, who better than landscaping experts to advise on the best ground conditions for landing and taking off?

All the Mawsons had to do was convince Weston Council that an aerodrome was definitely something a "pleasure resort" like Weston should be looking into.

More importantly, that flying was cost-efficient and safe.

Thankfully, wrote the Mawsons, in their 18-page report (kindly discovered and photocopied for me by the ever-helpful Nicki Bobette of Weston Library) there had only been "four accidents involving the death of passengers" on "the great air liners" since 1919.

And in the case of 'joy-rides' (or pleasure flights) there had only been "one fatal accident and this was due to a passenger falling out of the aeroplane".

"Indeed," they wrote, "the wonder is that there have not been more accidents due to the silliness of 'joy-riding' passengers". Like the incident in Lancaster when onlookers observed that "a passenger had left his seat and was crawling about the wings of the machine". It turned out he "was doing this for a silly bet".

But, basically, the Mawsons' advice was that modern flying is considered pretty safe and "up-to-date machines" are equipped to cover "practically every risk".

So, with the national passion for flying growing at such a rapid pace, they strongly recommended that Weston go ahead with "the only course possible under the circumstances", adopting a "virile alertness and up-to-dateness" to keep pace with other resorts.

Otherwise, they added, there's a serious "risk of being out of date" with "other more wide-awake municipalities scoring off us!"

Weston Aerodrome eventually opened eight years later in 1936 on Locking Moor. With half-hourly flights to Cardiff and flights abroad it became the second busiest civil airfield in the country before everything went pear-shaped on the outbreak of war.

What if Weston still had the second busiest airport in the country?

So Weston got its aerodrome and its place as the country's Number Two Airport, a position now held by Gatwick with over 34 million passengers on 263,653 planes in 2008 (according to Wikipedia).

Imagine, Weston residents with your relatively peaceful skies, if World War II had never happened and Weston Airport had remained up there as Number Two…

Recycling 1920s style

Around 1924, Weston's Town Surveyor, Harry Brown, was rummaging around in a garden in Croydon when he uncovered a 200-foot Portland Stone terrace (thought to be from Italy) complete with statues of the Four Seasons.

Excited, he fired off a letter to my Great Uncle Thomas Mawson's firm who were working on Weston's Winter Gardens.

The Mawsons were mulling over how to divide the rear of the Winter Gardens from the High Street. A clipped hedge seemed the obvious solution but it could take years to mature. The Portland Stone terrace, thought Harry Brown, was a take-out-of-the-box-and-go solution. All they had to do was find the cash, ship it to Weston, tweak the original plans so it looked right and put it in position.

So Mawson's son, Edward, rushed to meet Brown in Croydon where "lying in a maze of aeroplane engines, propellers and a large collection of War Office material awaiting disposal, I saw the magnificent Portland Stone terrace".

Milton quarry owner and future Weston Mayor, Henry Butt, provided the cash and the Winter Gardens got its Italian stone terrace which, said Edward Mawson talking to the Weston-Super-Mare Gazette, "I feel sure that if its late owner... could see it in its present position, he would feel that at last he had found a setting which showed it up to better advantage even than his wonderful garden".

Recycling 1920's style!

Hand me a brown paper bag pleeeeeease!

Inspired by the incredibly boring and technical report in my Dad's civil engineering magazine, I decided to check on how Weston's Grand Pier is progressing.

I'm intrigued to see that, according to the Weston Mercury, the new pavilion will have "a 4D cinema with its own weather system" featuring "moving seats and leg ticklers, alongside regular bursts of wind, rain and snow during films".

Does this mean the cinema will be open to the elements, I wonder? I go to the cinema to escape the bad weather, not to get more of it!

And what, in Heaven's name, is a 'leg tickler'?

Hopefully not the kind of 'leg tickler' I experienced at the *(Good Old Days)* Leeds City Varieties Music Hall the other month. During the show, something creepy crawled up inside my jeans and started feasting on my leg. By the time I got home I was covered in itchy red bites which lasted the whole weekend.

As for 4D… well 3D is bad enough. At Christmas we went to see *Avatar* at Bradford's IMAX cinema. Not my choice of movie, but it was my husband's and son's birthdays. So, teeth gritted, I agreed to go along.

Sitting on the second row, with the massive screen just feet from my face and the heavy 3D specs bearing down on my nose, the sensation was nauseating. I felt genuinely ill.

So the prospect of a similar experience on Weston's Grand Pier but in 4D with fighter-jet-simulator-style moving seats plus wind, rain, snow and something nasty tickling my leg… well… I think I'll give it a miss, thank you.

Especially if it's anything like the "typical 4D theatre" described on the Science Museum's website where "the seats pitch fore and aft, roll from side to side and heave up and down" and also "vibrate and drop" with "sensory effects" that "activate the senses" including wind, "distinct aromas" (??!!), water spray and - yes - our friends the mysterious leg ticklers.

Hand me a brown paper bag pleeeeeease!

And my 82-year old Mum agrees, nostalgically remembering an earlier state-of-the-art cinema experience in Weston: the Odeon's Compton organ rising out of the ground with flashing lights. "Now *that* was 3D cinema…"

But 4D nausea aside, it's interesting to see how the Grand Pier is progressing, even if Dad's civil engineering mag, like many other people, insist on referring to the burned down pavilion as Victorian

To Weston with love...

or Edwardian when you and I know it was a 1930's building.

Oh and while I'm in nit-picking mode, they kept referring to the burned down pavilion as Weston's old pier. Surely the Old Pier is a few hundred yards up the coast ...

Driving me mad

I see my pet hate, pay-and-display parking, has reared its ugly head again, this time with North Somerset Council planning to force Weston motorists to pay for parking until 10pm at night.

The reward? A laughing-all-the-way-to-the-bank £2million in profit!

I've touched on this subject before: the way you can park to your heart's content and for free in French seaside resorts, even bang on the seafront at the Cote d'Azur, yet here you're held for ransom every time you want to park.

But 10pm is taking the Michael.

Even in Leeds City Centre you can park for free after 6pm and all day Sunday and Bank Holidays. I just hope North Somerset Council isn't swapping ideas with Leeds. If we lose our free parking after 6, I'll know where to point the finger!

But what I object to even more than paying-and-displaying when I'm enjoying myself is paying-and-displaying when I'm NOT.

Like when I had to rush my son Ben to hospital the other week. These days it cost £1 an hour to park at Leeds hospitals. And, unlike

To Weston with love...

some hospitals that have a pay-on-exit system, you have to guess how long you're going to be.

And with the NHS, and especially A&E, who knows? So everyone ends up overpaying. "Yippee!" shouts the NHS Trust, laughing all the way to the bank.

But there's a new disease that's creeping onto our streets: Residents Only Parking. Suddenly roads where you used to park quite happily are Residents Only. Park within 10 miles of where you want to go and you'll get a ticket slapped on your windscreen.

Understandable, I guess, for residents who are probably sick to the back teeth of the likes of me parking outside their home, but crazy in areas where the residents don't appear to have any cars.

Like near the above Leeds hospital - a mass of run-down back-to-back houses with an equal mass of empty Residents Only car parking spaces.

Then ten miles up the road we encounter Harrogate and the mysteries of Disc Parking where it seems that no-one is welcome except carriers of the elusive Disc.

You can Enjoy Free Parking for two hours at Somerfields. Sorry, did someone say *enjoy* parking? Not when I'm grappling with a trolley that doesn't want to go where I want with contents that cost me a fortune when I get to the till followed by a trolley park that's miles away from my car, across speed bumps that my ten-ton trolley definitely doesn't want to negotiate. I might enjoy the bottle of wine I've bought to calm my nerves, but the parking - no.

Anyway, I digress. When my Grandparents lived in Weston in the

1960's and 70's they had a pass which entitled them to free parking virtually anywhere plus free access to the toll road to Kewstoke.

Mind you, in those days, you could park practically anywhere for free. My Dad always managed to get a prime parking place on the seafront outside the Marine Lake.

But these days, like I said before, I have my own secret parking place which I always make for when in Weston.

Mind you, no doubt the Council will have become wise to that and I'll have the double yellows or the ubiquitous pay-and-display (till 10pm) awaiting me next time I visit…

Granny's Somerset Easter Biscuits

In the 1950s, 60s and 70s in Weston there was nothing my Granny liked to do more than hold a tea party - and, boy, did she love to bake!

She and her Weston friends would swap recipes and Granny wrote down her favourites in an exercise book, not unlike those featured on the Hairy Bikers' recent *Mums Know Best* series.

All the old ladies lived on Weston hillside: Granny in Eastfield Park, her sister-in-law Hetty Schoon in Trewartha Park, cricket-mad Dorothy Taylor in Farm Road and Jessie Chaplain in Highbury Road.

For the moment I've picked out just one of the recipes and typed it up below. I was going to include more, but I wanted to try them out first. So watch this space, there will be more to come!

Whenever we visited Weston at Easter or in the spring, we'd be greeted by Granny Totty armed with a pot of tea and a plate of delectable Somerset Easter Biscuits.

Last weekend, I baked a batch. My son said the subtle taste of lemon made him think of a field full of daffodils.

So if you fancy a bit of retro baking, why not try out her recipe?
Note: the recipe uses imperial measurements.

Granny Totty's Somerset Easter Biscuits (makes around 20)

Ingredients: 8oz plain flour, 4oz butter, 4oz caster sugar, grated zest of one large lemon, 1/2 tsp baking powder, 1 egg, 2oz currants, extra sugar for sprinkling.

Preheat oven to gas mark 4 (180C). Rub the butter into the flour, add the sugar and lemon zest, baking powder and currants. Mix in the beaten egg. Roll out 1/4 inch thick and cut into biscuits with a fluted 3 inch cutter. Bake on a greased baking sheet for 18-20 minutes. When lightly golden, remove from oven and sprinkle with sugar while still hot.

I'm on my way to Weston!

Great news - my husband and son are spending bank holiday weekend doing blokey things like laying paving stones, planting spuds and sawing things up in the shed. So I've decided to take myself off to... Weston!

I've booked my accommodation. Now it's just a case of taking out a second mortgage to pay for the petrol and driving all that way.

So what will I do in Weston? Well, I'll take a look at the new Grand Pier. I had a quick peek on Facebook and it's looking a lot better than I thought it would.

I'll have a cappuccino in my favourite little café: the Cove Café at Anchor Head. And I'll put on some stout shoes to cope with all the walking, unlike last time when I was virtually crippled after walking up and down the prom plus my sentimental stroll along South Road to Eastfield Park and back, just like I used to do in the 1970s...

Will my Grandparents' flat still be empty and neglected? I always get butterflies when I go there - firstly because it's so sad to see it go to ruin and secondly because I'm worried someone will wonder what

I'm on my way to Weston!

the blazes I'm doing, staring at their house.

I might do a re-run of my train trip to Paignton and back, revisiting the weekly 'runabout' ticket we used to buy in the 70s. The other summer when I did it the weather was so atrocious I couldn't even walk across Torquay station car park for the driving wind and rain. And doing the coastal run by Dawlish was really scary with waves crashing over the track. A far cry from the sparkling blue sea in the red hot summer of 1976 when we'd leap off the train and virtually jump straight in the sea.

It will be the first time I've been in Weston since I discovered my Great Great Uncle was responsible for much of the Winter Gardens design back in the 1920s - so that will take on a whole new light. More photo opportunities... And finally (weather permitting), I'll watch the sun set over the sea - something we always used to do from the Prince Consort Gardens in the 1960s and 70s while sailing our little plastic boats on the old boating pond.

So that's what I'll be up to on May bank holiday weekend. And fingers crossed the sun will shine, at least for some of the weekend...

Otherwise I'm off to Bristol shopping.

Going off the rails

Weighing up the cost of petrol and the hassle of driving 225 miles and back over a bank holiday, I decided to take the train to Weston the other weekend.

Good decision? Not sure, really. It was quicker, but far from cheap (£90 return) or comfortable.

I never travel light, so lugging my suitcase on and off trains and doing my back in lifting it onto the luggage shelf wasn't brilliant. And it wasn't helped by someone dumping a huge case on top of mine, nearly squashing it, after sending it flying to the floor. Ouch, my laptop!!!

Then there's the fact that the Cross Country Train's crowded to bursting point - and the air conditioning doesn't seem to be working too well giving it that clammy aroma you get in an overheated, under-ventilated school classroom.

I've got one of those large businessmen sitting next to me who feels obliged to take up half my seat, arm rest and floor space as well as his own. Meanwhile he's checking what look like pointless spread sheets on his laptop, presumably in a bid to look 'important'.

Then there's the toilet... In the Bad Old Days of British Rail you got at least two toilets per coach, sometimes four. In those days coaches had fewer seats, before they introduced the cram-'em-in-like-sardines airline-style seating. So I counted around 76 seats with just one toilet serving them all. And that toilet was blocked and unusable.

So that meant two coaches of around 152 passengers in total (plus more standing) using just one, not very clean loo.

Not good.

Oh, and I discover that we are no longer 'passengers'; we are 'customers', apparently.

Well this particular customer isn't over the moon with the fact the train's so crowded the refreshments trolley can't make it down the aisles. So there's a 45-minute wait at what passes for a buffet car followed by an obstacle course over bikes, students and people sitting on luggage - plus those doors that don't open automatically, meaning you need a spare hand to press the button.

Then there's the connection from Bristol to Weston, like a bus on rails with me and my suitcase crammed into a corner by the draughty door for the duration.

The only saving grace is the taxi from Weston station with a very pleasant driver and an equally pleasant price (compared to Leeds taxis). But when you don't have a car you're limited to what you can do and where you can go. It's a 20-minute walk from the apartment I've rented to Tesco's and town - and then you have to lug your shopping back along a bleak, rainy, windswept promenade and up the steep Highbury Road.

To Weston with love…

Over the weekend I take the (20-minute walk to the station and the) train to the South Devon Coast. I have to change twice to get to Paignton and ditto on the way back, only when I get to Taunton the train is cancelled. An hour later it's cancelled again as are all trains to Weston, so I have to jump on a train to Bristol, which bypasses the Weston loop, and then wait for a connection back to Weston. And then there's the 20 minute walk back to the apartment. Phew!

And it isn't helped by the fact I've developed a dickey tummy, probably something I picked up from those train toilets…

Going back to Leeds, it's a taxi to Weston station followed by all change at Bristol again onto the Plymouth / Edinburgh train. With no less than 17 universities en route it's jam-packed with students. I feel very middle-aged…

There's an annoying student behind me on her mobile droning on about her weekend sessions in the sauna and on a water bed (too much information…). And the student in front of me seems to be receiving texts every five seconds, notified by an irritating little tune.

Again the problem of too many passengers for not enough toilets and so many suitcases piled on top of mine that I've got muscles like Charles Atlas by the time I've removed my case as we arrive back at Leeds.

Finally I take the bus home, followed by a 10-walk to my door. Door to door it's taken me nearly 6 hours, cost me over £100 and I'm absolutely knackered!

Motorway next time? You bet!

No-one addresses my Dad as "darling"...

I once met a man who used to work for my Dad. In his hay day Dad was Mains Drainage CEO for Leeds City Council and this guy used to quake with fear at Dad's approach, hiding under the desk until he had passed through the office.

Ex-boys' boarding school and army (World War II), Dad was very much 'old school' in his people-management and parenting skills. 'Victorian Dad' might be a good way to describe him.

Yet on good days, Dad could be great fun - and both he and I were very artistic and used to spend hours together on some creative project or other. Dad also made a mean snowman and he once handmade and painted the most amazing dolls house for my Christmas present.

It was always Dad who used to take us to the Marine Lake in Weston, building incredible structures in the pliable sand - a legacy of his civil engineering background, no doubt.

And it's because of Dad that we know Weston railway station and the train line to the South West Coast so well. Dad was a true 'train spotter'!

These days Dad is nearly 90. A shadow of his former physical self, he's lost none of his CEO mentality and his mind is still as sharp as a new pin.

So last weekend, when Dad was rushed into hospital with suspected pneumonia, I was horrified at the way the nursing staff treated him.

Whenever he spoke, they ignored him, probably assuming he'd lost his marbles and was rambling on when it was something that was very important to him.

He was very poorly, so talking wasn't easy. When a nurse did reply, it was to address him as "Darling" (no-one, ever, addresses my Dad as "Darling" - and imagine if the hide-under-the-desk employee had dared to do that!!) and to talk to him as if he were a child.

The sheer helpless look he threw at me will stay with me for life. Dad has never looked at me like that and in a curious way I found it extremely touching.

You see, Dad and I have never had a close father-daughter relationship and it's something that's made me sad over the years.

But the older he gets, the more I realise that someone of his generation, and with his male-orientated boarding school / army background, almost certainly finds it very hard to relate to women and express his feelings.

More and more these days, I realise that it's probably something he'd love to be able to do. Maybe as he moves into his 90s, we'll make up for all those lost years.

Last weekend, however, seeing him very ill in hospital (his first hospital visit since he had kidney stones removed in the 1970s), I wondered whether he'd make the end of this week, let alone his 90s... Which brought back all the good memories of Dad when we were kids; I even found myself looking tearfully through all his old 35mm slides, many of which are of Dad and me in Weston.

But thankfully Dad is on the mend. And I hope that no-one ever again talks to him like a child or calls him "Darling".

Rooms

I'm in a Victorian villa apartment on Weston hillside, propped up in bed drinking in the amazing view across the Bay towards Uphill Church and Brean Down.

Through the left-hand window I can see the old Knightstone Theatre and Baths and through the right-hand window, the new apartments tagged on the end a couple of years back.

But the reason I like this room so much is that (apart from the incredible view) it's virtually a carbon-copy of the bedroom I used at my Grandparents' flat in Eastfield Park.

It's the same shape and size, even the door and fireplace are in the same place. The fire surround is identical, no doubt one of thousands churned out in Weston during the late 19th century.

Ditto the stunning cast-iron fireplace and grate with its pretty arch with cast-iron bird on a cast-iron branch, with pretty grey, black and white patterned tiles on either side. Unfortunately in Granny's flat the cast-iron bit was boxed in by a sheet of plywood with a characterless electric fire in front. So I never got to see what was hidden behind. An identical cast-iron bird, maybe?

I'd forgotten just how massive these rooms are. You'd need a high stepladder just to change a light bulb, let alone to paint the ceiling. Like the stepladder I saw yesterday in the above-mentioned bedroom in Granny's old flat. Whoever owns the flat seems to have been playing around with it for years because every time I take a nosy look, the windows are curtainless and there seems to be some kind of DIY work going on.

Maybe when they started they didn't realise what a mammoth task it would be - in which case I totally forgive them, provided they haven't ripped out the wonderful original features, like the Victorian fireplaces or the panelled doors complete with wonderful brass handles.

The problem with these flats is that they're often difficult to convert into something that's usable by modern standards. My Grandparents had to make lots of compromises when they got in the builders to do their conversion back in the 1950s.

The staircase to the attic rooms was cut off around a metre from the floor below, meaning you needed a small stepladder to climb onto the first stair. The kitchen was tiny, the bathroom long and narrow, yet the (windowless) landing was vast.

In the apartment I'm staying in this weekend, the bathroom is dark and windowless - another casualty of the conversion into flats. And the external staircase goes straight up and over the original elegantly arched entrance porch - obviously a tricky problem the builder never managed to solve successfully.

Inside, it's interesting to work out what the original room layout would have been which you can do by looking at the coving along the ceiling. In the case of this apartment, it's cut off by a recent wall and then continues in the kitchen on the other side. Once these would have been one huge room.

It's also interesting to think just how many more people must live in these converted properties than in the original houses.

I instinctively know what my former mains drainage engineer Dad would think…

He'd wonder about how the 19th century sewers could cope with double, treble or quadruple the number of toilets, baths and showers!

What's been going on in Weston?

As a child I loved to build roads and cityscapes on Weston's beach - and now it seems dozens of contractors are doing the same. Only this time they're doing it on the Marine Lake / Winter Gardens section of the promenade, around Regent Street and on the Grand Pier.

I've just spent a long weekend in Weston, in an apartment up above the Marine Lake with a fantastic view!

It's funny seeing Weston in such a visible state of change. The last Big Change was after the 1980s storms which wrought havoc at the Marine Lake and which hasn't been the same ever since.

In fact they seem to have been doing work there since my son was a baby - and he's 16 now.

Anyway, I spent the weekend dodging the cordoned-off bits of prom and walking along the new paved section with its new wall (which doesn't quite match the old sea wall that runs parallel to it).

I was curious to see how the Grand Pier has progressed. I've kept up to date with its page on Facebook, etc but it's kind of weird to see it 'in the flesh' so to speak when you're used to seeing the old

To Weston with love...

structure. I thought I'd hate it, but I'm giving it a good 9 out of 10. Really, it's not too bad at all. I just hope it weathers well.

Back in the 1920s people were equally as curious about the new Winter Gardens - when my Gt Gt Uncle and his team moved in to level Roger's Field.

His son, Edward Mawson, said: "...there was never a moment from quite early in the morning to late in the evening when the work was without its crowd of interested spectators..."

This weekend I also took a closer look at the antique stone terrace which Gt Gt Uncle helped to salvage from a garden in Croydon.

It's always been there, of course. It's just that I never knew about the Mawson involvement or the fact it's so old.

The local paper at the time quoted Edward Mawson as saying, "I feel sure that if its late owner... could see it in its present position, he would feel that at last he had found a setting which showed it up to better advantage even than his wonderful garden".

Not so these days, unfortunately... Not with the graffiti that's been sprayed on it.

Nor the municipal block paving that's replaced the gardens and tennis courts which the Mawsons worked so tirelessly to clear of the 1920s equivalent of Japanese Knot Weed.

Nor the soulless Sovereign Shopping Centre with its cheap imitation of the Winter Gardens' architectural theme.

Nor all the ever-present trodden-in chewing gum underfoot (councils spend a fortune on pedestrianisation just to end up with squashed blobs of this stuff everywhere).

Plus I couldn't help but notice there's an awful lot of doggy-doos underfoot in Weston, too. (A far cry from my 'hippy' days of the mid-1970s when Weston pavements were clean enough for me to walk barefoot.)

But the front of the Winter Gardens and Grand Pier are looking good - and I'm sure that, once I get used to it, the new paved, walled-in prom will look reasonably OK too.

It's built to keep the sea out. Let's hope it will also keep irresponsible dog owners, graffiti 'artists' and gum-chewing louts out, too.

Demolition-happy

Was the planner that gave permission for the Knightstone apartments related to the one that gave the go-ahead for Weston Technical College back in 1970, I wonder?

A close cousin, maybe, of the other planner who said "Yes" to demolishing the diving stage in the 1937 Open Air Pool and gave the go-ahead to convert it into the 1980s Tropicana, obviously 'the future' in terms of seaside leisure attractions?

A brother, perhaps, of the planner who said "Yes" to the bulldozers that levelled the quaint Glentworth Hall opposite the Marine Lake and replaced it with Glentworth Court Flats (which look uncannily similar to what's going on at the end of the Knightstone)? Plus umpteen other 'improvements' and demolitions I've noticed in my years in Weston that weren't caused by WWII bombs or storm damage.

The trouble is, time has shown that these modern buildings don't age well. While Dr Fox's Bath House, the Knightstone Baths (where I learned to swim) and the Knightstone Theatre have aged relatively gracefully (with a little help from restorers), they could easily be

Demolition-happy

marred in 20 years' time by the block of 'noughties' flats at the rear… This is my opinion, at any rate.

If it were me, I'd have chosen one of those architects that are good at reproducing traditional styles - the kind where you can't actually tell where the original building ends and the new one begins. Not the pastiche styling adopted by the Sovereign Shopping Centre architect, but something that mirrors the Baths or the Theatre and ages equally well.

And while I'm on this subject… what are the plans for Birnbeck Pier? Are there indeed any plans? To me, that area of Weston is the most picturesque and genteel. Or at least it was once…

Sure, the Prince Consort Gardens still have their manicured lawns, beautifully kept flower beds and pretty lily pond (if you ignore the cider can floating alongside the ducks).

Behind, developers are making a sterling effort at restoring the elegant mansions overlooking the Bay, but unfortunately also overlooking the twisted shell of the burned-out Royal Pier Hotel and the decaying Birnbeck Pier.

How long will the Pier stay a decaying, ghostly ruin with - as can be seen from various photographs on the Net - derelict reminders of its lively past still weathering the storms that hit that vulnerable section of the Bristol Channel?

If it were me I'd restore it as a museum of piers of days gone by. A bit like they've done with the SS Great Britain at Bristol.

People could promenade up and down, see the clock, hear the old organ being played, have a dance in the dancehall and maybe get on a real paddle steamer to Barry Island just like we used to do once upon a time.

The only problem - and it is one of the major reasons why the pier went into decline in the first place - is that Birnbeck Pier is so far off the 'beaten tourist track'. And now there are no boats to Wales, packed with coalminers keen on a thrills-and-spills day out on Weston's historic pier, how would they get the tourists to 'brave' that neglected, unfashionable part of Weston?

When life was so much simpler...

I picked up a 1958 map of Weston in a York charity shop yesterday. (Curiously, they had several copies.) And doesn't Weston look smaller?

In those pre Dr (Branch-Lines-Vandal) Beeching days you could catch a train from Yatton to Clevedon and, the other way, to Winscombe, Axebridge, Cheddar, Wells and beyond. Highbridge really was 'for Burnham-on-Sea', with trains to Glastonbury in the opposite direction. And, of course, there was no M5 motorway carving up the terrain.

Suddenly it occurred to me that life must have been so much simpler back then. People would talk to each other in the street and on the (steam) train rather than gabbing down their mobile phones or viewing others with suspicion.

There were no thousands of emails to distract you, just typed or hand-written letters, only written when necessary rather than firing one off every few seconds. Granny Totty used to take great pleasure in sitting at her writing table overlooking Weston Bay, carefully writing letter after letter to her friends across the globe.

There was no cyber-crime with people trying to 'phish' for your credit card or bank details - or trying to compromise your website. And of course there were no websites. In those days you researched information down at the library, in encyclopaedias or you sent off for information in the post. Viruses were something you caught and drugs were what you took for an illness.

And you waited for things patiently.

In a day and age before everyone rushed around in a mega whirlwind of stress you waited for the post to arrive. You waited for the bus or train. You waited for telephone calls, if you had a phone. And if you didn't, you waited in the queue at the local phone box. You waited to be served at your local grocer, bakery, butcher or whatever. (Granny Totty did her grocery shopping in Meadow Street.) You waited for things to be delivered or ordered - or you just did without. And I expect you spent a lot less.

Oh I don't doubt there were stresses in life. Medical treatments weren't as far advanced, for example, so you could suffer from more ailments for longer. And cancer cures were few and far between.

Feminism was still in its infancy, so as a married woman and mother I may have found it harder to work, let alone run my own business and let alone run it from home using the internet! (I remember my Mum telling me how thrilled Granny Totty was as a young woman when the Great War enabled her to work in a hospital dispensary; other than that her father refused to allow her to work at all.) And I couldn't pick up my car keys every time I wanted to go

When life was so much simpler...

out. Like my Mum in 1958, I'd walk to the local shops or get delivery boys to deliver stuff.

But while I was at the shops I'd chat to friends and neighbours. I'd know the shopkeepers by name ('Mr Blight the chemist', for example, with his Victorian pharmacy interior complete with those giant clear tear-shaped jars full of mysterious coloured liquids or 'Mr Morrison, the greengrocer'.)

1958 was the year I was born. The following summer was my first summer in Weston, travelling there by sooty black steam train from Leeds.

In those days my Grandparents wouldn't think twice about leaving their front door not simply unlocked, but wide open. They never experienced any crime.

You could still park on the seafront for free - and find a car parking space easily. The toilets on the Knightstone still welcomed you to Weston-Super-Mare in lights, you could buy a knickerbocker glory in Fortes ice cream parlour and enjoy the Model Railway above the (still colonnaded) Marine Lake. You could still catch a coach from the coach station on the seafront and watch county cricket in Clarence Park. And you could still learn to swim in the Knightstone Baths, relax at the Rozel bandstand and catch a paddle steamer to Barry Island from an intact Birnbeck Pier.

So here I am, rose-coloured spectacles well and truly on, looking at a map of Weston in 1958 that's as crisp and new as if it were printed yesterday. And by the way, I'm coming down to Weston in a few days' time - my second visit this year. Care of the motorways, of

To Weston with love…

course. In 1958 it would have been by train. But, after my experience with Cross Country Trains earlier this year, I prefer to drive.

My second visit to Weston this year

I see the prom is nearly finished, although I'm not convinced by the new wall between it and the road. It's lost that famous 'open' feel and, try as they might, the new wall doesn't match the old wall, even with its fake 'weathered' look on the top.

And whose idea was that arch? Maybe you love it, but I'm not sure what it's saying to me. A 'gateway' to the prom? But why there? And why so stark and boxy? Like something out of a theatre or an *It's a Knockout* set.

I don't think it could have been designed by the same person as that android bus thing in Meadow Street. That has a surreal kind of elegance to it, even if it would look more at home on Mars.

I'm not sure, either, about the slabs of stone dumped around the prom for people to sit on. What's wrong with reproducing the Victorian seats at the Madeira Cove? Weston is an elegant Victorian seaside resort, after all. (So why not make the aforementioned arch elegant, too? Say, in wrought iron rather than stone?)

To Weston with love...

Also, with the old prom, the land train track was clearly marked so you could make sure you kept well out of the way. Now you're constantly looking over your shoulder to make sure it's not creeping up on you.

I'm still disappointed by what they did some years ago around the back of the Winter Gardens / Sovereign Shopping Centre area, all but destroying the landscaping created by my Great Great Uncle Mawson in the 1920s.

And no-one can help the result of the 1980s storms on the Marine Lake. It never did fully recover and it's a real shame they can't reproduce the original colonnades and iron railings. Plus, I'm sure the shoreline has moved almost 90 degrees from where it used to be.

However the new Knightstone flats are growing on me - and I see they're restoring the stonework at the front of the old Baths. And the new causeway is a vast improvement on the old one.

So - all in all - Weston's looking ten times smarter than it did a few years back, even if Tropicana, the Royal Pier Hotel and the Old Pier are still derelict. And even if the Grand Pier isn't open yet - and the beach lawns around the Regent Street area are still a work in progress.

2013 - Update

While I was writing my blog for the Weston Mercury, my teenage son developed a serious illness: Anorexia Nervosa. You can see one or two references to what was happening to our family in the preceding chapters. However, at the time, I preferred to keep this awful news private - and to keep my Weston blog relatively upbeat.

Towards the end of 2010 I stopped writing the Weston blog - for two reasons. Firstly, my son's illness was taking over our lives completely and I simply didn't have the time or energy to write the blog. And secondly, it must have been around then that the Weston Mercury stopped having an online blog.

However in the following chapter I've included a post I never submitted, explaining why I'd been a bit elusive on the blogging front for a while at the end of 2009.

I still kept up the Weston blog throughout most of 2010, although it was difficult to give it my undivided attention. However over this distressing period the town of Weston-Super-Mare provided an occasional solace for me as I sought to 'escape' from my son's illness now and again, and took myself off for a few days to the little self-catering apartment on Weston's hillside which I describe in some of the preceding chapters.

Then, in summer 2011, as my son began to slowly recover, I took him down to Weston with me, to that apartment. I have a fabulous photograph of my son, Ben, standing on a rock at Anchor Head, looking triumphant as - through his own strong will and determination - he fought to overcome the devastating mental illness that had trapped him for two years.

I remember us both standing in the Prince Consort Gardens later that evening, watching the sun go down behind Birnbeck Pier, turning the muddy Bristol Channel a beautiful gold, just as I used to do with my Grandparents. And I knew that, although there was still some way to go - and, in the event, it took another eighteen months or so - my son was on the way back to health.

Then, in the summer of 2013, we went to Weston again; indeed I visited Weston on three occasions that year. On the first, I did the familiar walk, along South Road and Cecil Road from Atlantic Road. I had a peek over the wall at my Grandpa's old vegetable garden and was sad to see that it was still in a state of extreme neglect and my favourite of the two potting sheds - the one with the whitewashed walls and potted plants on the window sills - was missing. I expect it had fallen down; last time I was there it looked as if it was on its last legs.

Around the front, very little had changed since my last visit - or indeed any of the visits described in this book. The flat still looked empty and unloved, which was so terribly sad.

So I walked back to the Marine Lake, via Lower Church Road and my Grandparents' church. And when I returned to Leeds I wrote the blog post you can read at the end of this book, this time in my other blog, the blog which I began in January 2011 to help other families struggling with anorexia.

December 2009 - Everything in our family has changed

I can't remember exactly when it joined our family. I think it was about late September, although looking back there were signs it was already present in the summer when my 15-year old son, Ben, started exercising more and carefully watching what he ate.

It's one of the reasons why I had a break from this blog for a while as our family life underwent a complete shift from being a normal family to being a family coping with anorexia.

With anorexia it's as if someone else moves into your head. Someone that taunts you all the time, telling you you're fat and unattractive, and you'll never be popular until you do something about it.

It has you pinching the skin on your skinny stomach, taunting you that it's rolls of fat. It makes you exercise like mad and examine yourself in the mirror critically. It makes you hate what you see.

It lies to you that it can make you ultra-handsome, ultra-slim and ultra-confident. It lies that it can put you in control. And part of this control is to control exactly what goes into your stomach, how much

December 2009 - Everything in our family has changed

of it and when. The minute you deviate from this rigid eating pattern, it lies to you that you're out of control. Just one serving of dinner that's not the 'right size' and it can have the sufferer banging their head on the fridge door and screaming.

I know, because that's what Ben was doing last night. And over the past three or four months we've watched him totally transform, physically and mentally.

I was in two minds as to whether to reveal our Big Problem in this blog - and of course I got Ben's permission to do it first. But we decided that anything that might help other families, and possibly the sufferers themselves, had to be a 'Good Thing'.

I can't possibly go into detail here, in this one entry. Over the past few months this thing has become SO HUGE that it's taken over most of my thoughts. It has taken over Ben. It has taken over our family.

And anorexia isn't just about eating; it's about a whole load of other symptoms that go with it - like depression, panic, zero self-esteem, etc. I don't just mean feeling a bit 'down' now and again, I mean deep, dark depression and self-hatred.

So what are we doing about it?

Believe it or not, we had to talk our GP into referring Ben to the local NHS adolescent mental health services for treatment. Then we found the waiting list was going to be 18 weeks or so - AFTER we'd received a letter from them which took a month to come through.

So there we were in November watching our son getting thinner and more depressed, but no-one to go to for help. If we are lucky the appointment may come through by Easter! Thankfully we have a bit of private health insurance we can use towards a private therapist. It's not the full all-on anorexia treatment; it's just a kind of stop-gap, if you like, until the real McCoy comes along.

This Christmas I thought about all those parents everywhere who, at Christmas, want - more than anything - to get their 'little boy' or 'little girl' back, whether it's drugs, runaways, gangs, crime, drinks, going off the rails or worse.

I want my 'little boy' back with his confident, outgoing personality and athletic physique. Looking at family photographs is painful, an instant reminder of what he used to look like and should look like, but doesn't anymore.

I have a thin waif for a son who is starting to look like a concentration camp victim and whose mood is so volatile I'm frightened every time I pick him up from school for fear of how his day has been. And, of course, mealtimes are even worse…

'They' tell me it can be cured. But when it's as massive as this I wonder if it will take a miracle.

For any parent, seeing your child suffer is one of the most excruciating and painful things you will ever face. It's even worse when the illness is a mental illness like anorexia nervosa that makes your child fight against you and against recovery. I just wish there was a magic pill he could take and - Hey Presto! - the old Ben would come back.

I can tell you, we've been keeping the Kleenex manufacturers in business!

2013 - Just me, a park, some wood pigeons and a squirrel

In 2011, as my son began the very slow road to recovery from anorexia, I began another blog - this time aimed at families of boys with eating disorders. I still write this blog which led to a number of books on the subject of eating disorders.

In my book *Please eat... A mother's struggle to free her teenage son from anorexia*, which describes our journey through anorexia, I talk about how - during the most stressful moments of my son's eating disorder - I'd take time out at the end of the garden to watch the vegetables grow. We have a long garden, so it was a fantastic way to truly 'walk away' from the nightmare of the eating disorder, even if it was only for a moment or two.

However there was another place, a place I'd imagine myself going to on those frequent nights when sleep evaded me. In summer 2013 I went back there - to the real place, and wrote about the experience in my blog anorexiaboyrecovery.blogspot.co.uk. The Secretary of the Eastfield Park Committee must have found it because she left a lovely comment on my blog.

To Weston with love…

This is a copy of that blog post:

There is an old Victorian metal gate set into limestone walls. It leads into a beautiful private park - the park opposite my late Grandparents' former house on the hillside at Weston-Super-Mare. Because it's a private park for residents only, tucked away in a very secluded part of Weston's hillside, there was never anyone there. Except me. And I used to love being the other side of that wall, in that park, surrounded by manicured rose bushes and shrubs, and grass covered with daisies.

During those anxiety-ridden sleepless nights at the height of my son's illness, the only way I could get to sleep was to escape from reality. I'd imagine myself going up to that old gate, opening it, walking through and closing it again. Once inside the park, I was cut off from the outside world. I was safe.

I'd use a technique where I'd imagine what the grass felt beneath my bare feet. I'd make a daisy chain, carefully examining each petal. And I'd gradually make my way through the park, listening to the wood pigeons with the sound of seagulls in the distance. Usually I'd fall asleep before I reached the gap in the wall which led up to my Grandparents' house in the tiny private cul-de-sac with its handsome 19th century villas.

Yesterday - in July 2013 - I went back to that park. And, unlike last time I went there, I ignored the 'private' sign on that gate, opened it and walked through the park again. Just like I used to do when I was a teenager, many, many years before the anorexia invaded

2013 - Just me, a park, some wood pigeons and a squirrel

our lives - a private, peaceful place where I felt safe and secure. And, just like in my imaginings, I kicked off my flip-flops and felt the grass beneath my feet, even if it was tinder-dry and parched by the 2013 summer heat. And I knew that I wouldn't care if anyone challenged me about trespassing in the private Eastfield Park.

But they didn't, because - just as it always used to be - there was just me.

And the wood pigeons and the odd squirrel.

Acknowledgements

Firstly, thank you to the Weston Mercury for allowing me to blog for them for two years, despite living many hundreds of miles away. Thank you to Weston Library's Nicki Bobette for providing a mountain of photocopies of documents and local newspaper reports from the 1920s, and for being generally helpful. I would like to thank Allen Cotton for providing information about his father, a pupil at Weston's Lewisham School, Weston historian Brian Austin and everyone else who contacted me with interesting snippets of information as a result of my appeals on the Weston Mercury website and my blog. Thank you to my Mum for sharing her memories of Weston in the 1930s and to the Somerset Archives at Taunton for providing copies of the 1940s plans to convert 9 Eastfield Park into flats. Thank you to the lady from the Eastfield Park residents' committee who contacted me via my current blog when she read the post about the squirrels and wood pigeons. Finally thank you to you, the reader, for showing an interest in my nostalgic ramblings about Weston!

Find out more at: www.bevmattocks.co.uk

By the same author

Please Eat... A Mother's Struggle To Free Her Teenage Son From Anorexia - a first-person account of Bev Mattocks' teenage son's recovery from anorexia, from his mother's perspective.

When Anorexia Came To Visit: Families Talk About How An Eating Disorder Invaded Their Lives – Bev Mattocks talks to 20 UK families about their experiences of dealing with an eating disorder.

Flairs, France & Serious Fashion Crimes: My 1975 Teenage Diary – Bev Mattocks' teenage diary from the 1970s, a must-read for anyone who was a teenager in the 1970s and 1980s, including - of course - references to Weston-Super-Mare!

The above books are available on Amazon and as Kindle downloads.

Find out more at: www.bevmattocks.co.uk
Or 'like' my Facebook page, where you can also see lots of family photos of Weston: *Love Weston-Super-Mare*

Printed in Great Britain
by Amazon